The Overland Journals

The
Overland
Journals
of
William and Charles Frush

by

William Frush and Charles Frush

Ye Galleon Press
Fairfield, Washington
2000

Library of Congress Cataloging-in-Publication Data

The overland journals of William and Charles Frush / by William Frush and Charles Frush.

p. cm.

Includes The overland diary...by William H. Frush and two diaries, A trip from The Dalles...and A trip from Fort Owens...by Charles W. Frush.

Includes index.

ISBN 0-87770-302-7 -- ISBN 0-87770-723-5 (pbk.)

1. Frush, Wm. H. (William H.)--Diaries. 2. Frush, Charles W.--Diaries. 3. Pioneers--West (U.S.)--Diaries. 4. West (U.S.)--Description and travel. 5. Overland Trails--Description and travel. 6. Overland journeys to the Pacific. 7. Frontier and pioneer life--West (U.S.) I. Frush, Wm. H. (William H.) Overland diary detailing his trip across the plains to Oregon with observations on the country passed through, sketches of the route and information and advice to emigrants on the Overland Trail, May 15-September 25, 1850. II. Frush, Charles W. Trip from The Dalles of the Columbia, Oregon, to Fort Owen, Bitter Root Valley, Montana, in the spring of 1858. III. Frush, Charles W. Trip from Fort Owens in the Bitter Root Valley to Fort Benson, on the Missouri River in the winter of 1858.

F593.O95 2000

979'.04'0922--dc21

[B]   00-043610

THE OVERLAND DIARY

DETAILING HIS TRIP ACROSS THE PLAINS TO
OREGON WITH OBSERVATIONS ON THE
COUNTRY PASSED THROUGH, SKETCHES OF
THE ROUTE AND INFORMATION AND ADVICE
TO EMIGRANTS ON THE OVERLAND TRAIL

May 15 - September 25, 1850

By

WM. H. FRUSH

YE GALLEON PRESS
FAIRFIELD, WASHINGTON

May 15th (1850) Left my family and home near Newark, Knox County, Missouri for California on one horse with the expectation of overtaking on route my brother with teem, John H. Frush.

May 20th. At 9 Ock arrived in St. Joseph, Mo., making 200 miles travel in a few hours over 5 days with a pack of 40 lb. besides myself.

May 21st. Remained in St. Joseph at Mansion House.

May 22nd. Wrote to my wife, and at 9 Ock crossed the Mo. River and traveled about 25 miles on route and at dark struck camp near a fine stream water that crosses road. Thare is Indian cornfields near. Thare is two in company of us, a Mr. Church of Hannibal, Mo. This is 5 miles East of the Indian Agency. Road good; grass & water plenty.

May 23rd. Called at the Agency & see Jno. Ferman & Brother and Col. Wm. P. Richardson, agents and my old friends. Traveled 30 odd miles this day and camped on plains with a single waggoner. Roads good, grass do & plenty water. See many dead horses and cattle, and several Teems going back from friend(s) dying.

May 24th. Cross River Mine Craw (Nemaha) at 12 Ock.m., and graze our horses on plains 2 miles west. Camped with 2 teems from Bee Town, Grant Co., Wis. Rod(e) 30 odd miles this day. All well.

May 25th. Sat'y. Started 6½ A.M. on route. Dined 12 miles E of B(ig) Blue. Made Big Blue 6 P.M. Found it not fordable. Camped at foot of Elm Tree all night. Distance from St. Joseph 130 miles. Roads fine.

May 26th. Sunday, Paid $1 to have my horse swam alongside of raft; 30c to gat my baggage and self ferried in a leather Bottomd boat. Left on route at 11 Ock and travel'd 22 miles and camp'd with some men from Ohio. They tented us. Left at Big Blue from 100 to 150 teems.

May 27th. Monday. Met a train of waggons from Fort Lareme owned by traders, also the Government Mail 9 Ock, A.M. Distance from St. Joseph about 160 miles at fine Branch spring running water & plenty timber. Dined 6m. west Branch spring & timber. See 5 graves near former Branch, part died '49. 5 m. further cross Sandy Creek, 10 ft wide 6 in deep; running pirty. Much roaling ground for 15 m. travel. Campt 18 miles East little Blue River with Co. from Decalb, Mo.

May 28th. Tuesday. 4 miles from camp met with Holliday, of Shelby Co., Mo., at the grave of Wm. Fisher of Knox Co., his Brother o'law. 11 Ock saw small herds Buffalowe and at this time fell in with Geo. Parker of Hannibal Co., packing. Joined them. 12 Oclk made little Blue; dined. Travel 15 miles & campt at 15 m. after 5 Ock. Roads fine all day. Roling ground; plenty grass & water for stock. Passed many teems. A train always in sight.

May 29th. Wed. Traveled all day up little Blue River. Many deep sandy revene putting into bottom. Roads fine. The sandy bottoms on this river here is full of Prickle Pears. But little timber or plenty of willow. Passes in this days travel 150 teems. 9 of us in company. All well. Some of the trains had fine sport after Buffalow to day. They killed one. The land here is vary sandy, but vary good to this river, and would produce well. Struck camp on this river to night.

May 30th. Thursday. Traveled 3 miles further up Blue River, then took to the devide for Platte River. Branch & water for stock in 6 miles; do 4 miles further. Some wood on boath. Travel 15 miles on vary level Prairie without wood or water, then come to sand bluffs—dry & deep sand—5 miles from Platte. Crossed bottom to bank of River & campt. No wood on south side. Some on Grand Island opposite. 18 miles now below Fort Karney. From St. Joseph 300 miles. Plenty of grass on bottom, and a number of teems traveling in sight and in camp. Water in River vary muddy & rapid. This is only a slough of main river 100 yds. wide.

May 31st. Friday. Left camp Early. Traveled 3 miles up River and at old camp got wood and took breakfast. Wrote a letter to my wife. All well. Good water here to drink in wells dug 3 ft. deep. Arrived at Fort Karney 12 Ock. Left at 1 Ock. Left letter in Fort. This is a new Fort near where Fort Childs was, on South side of River ½ mile off & 4 miles from the head of Grand Island, 425 miles from St. Joseph. Camped 6 miles w. of Fort on river bank. No timber all day. Fell in with D. Fisher's co. Thare has bin plenty Antilope and Buffalow for 150 miles back.

June 1st. Sat'y. Left camp 7 Ock. Rode 4 hours and dined 18 miles above Fort. No timber. 10 miles from Fort timber near road on Island. 8 miles further plenty timber on Island near road easy come at. Here I see Robt Brown of Lewis Co., Mo. Camped 22 miles above Fort. Jno. Gidin of Shelby Co., Mo. take with Colera after dark. I went for Dr. Brown at his camp, took him to see him in night erly. He cramped and purged vary much during night. Night rainy and stormy. I lay outside tent all night in rain. Next morning I breakfasted with Dr. Brown and took him to see patient again. Dr. charge $2.

June 2. Sunday. Left Parker & Co. at camp and left alone on route. Jno. Gidin vary bad. I had no hopes of him. Travel alone thinking it not prudent to stay. Travel about 30 miles, and fell in with Wm. Fore, Jarvis, August Easton, Vanoy and others from Palmyra, and Griff Brisintine & others from New London—stay with them. Supt and breakfasted next morning. 3 or 4 died on the road in this days travel, said of Colera. One, ½ mile from this camp left wife & 9 children helpless. They had not moved when I left.

June 3rd. Monday. Left camp and found water and Timber on main shore in 17 miles. This is the first above Fort Karney and about 75 miles. Passed Sinclair with cattle here. Campt with Gent'n from Platte Co., Mo. at head of sand bluffs. Traveled 34 or 5 miles to day. Near this, road leaves River & cuts bend on high ground. No wood or water to crossing of S. Fork Platte, 20 miles. Take wood from River & 2 Branches that you cross when you strike the first high ground 90 or 100 miles above Fort Karney. Passed many teems to day. Traveled alone all day. Well.

June 4th Tuesday. Traveled 20 miles and Forded Platte River by 11½ Ock A.M. This River is here all in one channel and ½ mile wide, about 18 inches deep. Lower banks are vary sandy bottom—water vary muddy and not a stick of timber in sight. Grazed my horse on north side. Took up South fork 10 miles. Grass. Crossed ridge to North fork 2 miles & camped on Bottom. Good grass for 5 miles. Stay this night with Col. Lee of Indiana & his train of outfit of 40. He treated me well with tent and Sup'r & Breakfast. Distance said from Fort to Crossing, 123 miles. No wood in days travel of 32 miles.

June 5th. Wednesday. From Col. Lee camp on 5 mile Bottom took ridge between rivers & kept it for 15 miles before come to N. Fork. No grass, timber or water. Decended bluff and struck river. Poor grass for 6 miles, no wood; do to camp. Pass Johnson of Lewis Co., Mo. and conversed with him. No grass to camp for 4 miles; 4 miles good. First 4 miles R(oad) runs near River, heavy & sandy; 2 miles poor grass; 4 miles to point. Sand Hill good (place) to camp. Campt in here with Baldwin & Co., Clinton Co., Mo. Traveled this day 35 miles. No wood. Plenty from here to Castle Bluff for Emigrants (for) a few years.

June 6th. Thursday. 2 miles to point hill 1 mile heavy sand; 2 miles bottom at Lower end; Ceder grove in center high on bluff. Good spring on side road & ceder trees. Leave River and take steep bluff 2 miles to deep sandy hollow. Down hollow—Ash Hollow this—to River 2 miles. Timber & springs. Mouth of hollow to Castle Tower 8 miles. Narrow dry bottom and sandy. Quicksand, alkili bottom 2 miles long & wide. Indians camp'd here as I passed at 12 Ock. Camped on dry sandy creek—some water. Indians plenty. Traveled 35 miles. Some heavy roads & Alkili swamps. Road runs near River. No wood for 80 miles—grass in places ever(y) 4 or 5 miles.

June 7th. Friday. Made Chimney Rock. Distance from Castle Rock 64 miles. Good roads generally this day. Plenty water & generally grass never more than 4 or 5 miles apart. Court House Rock & creek of good running water 30 ft wide, 10 in deep, 13 miles before you reach Chimney Rock. Passed Jacob Righter & R. Meyers, Jo Poter & Co., at 12 Ock this day. Camp'd with Mr. S. Stalcup & Wm Dor of Shelby Co., Mo. Vary good camping for 6 miles. No wood.

June 8th. Saturday. Traveled from 6 miles East of Chimney Rock to 6 miles west Scotts bluffs, 33 miles. From Chimney Rock to Scotts Bluffs, 20 miles. 1st 10 miles good grass, road near river. R(oad) leaves river then and poor grass to creek 12 miles west Scotts Bluff. Cold spring west end Scotts Bluff. This Bluff and other surrounding, forming a great basin between them and affording a vary Romantic scenery. You pass through basin and leave the Bluff next river. Much Red Seeder & pine nots on basin; look as if it was floorwood. None growing only on cliffes. Lay in wood here and at bluff. Indian village and Smith Shop temperally at spring on bluff refer'd to above.

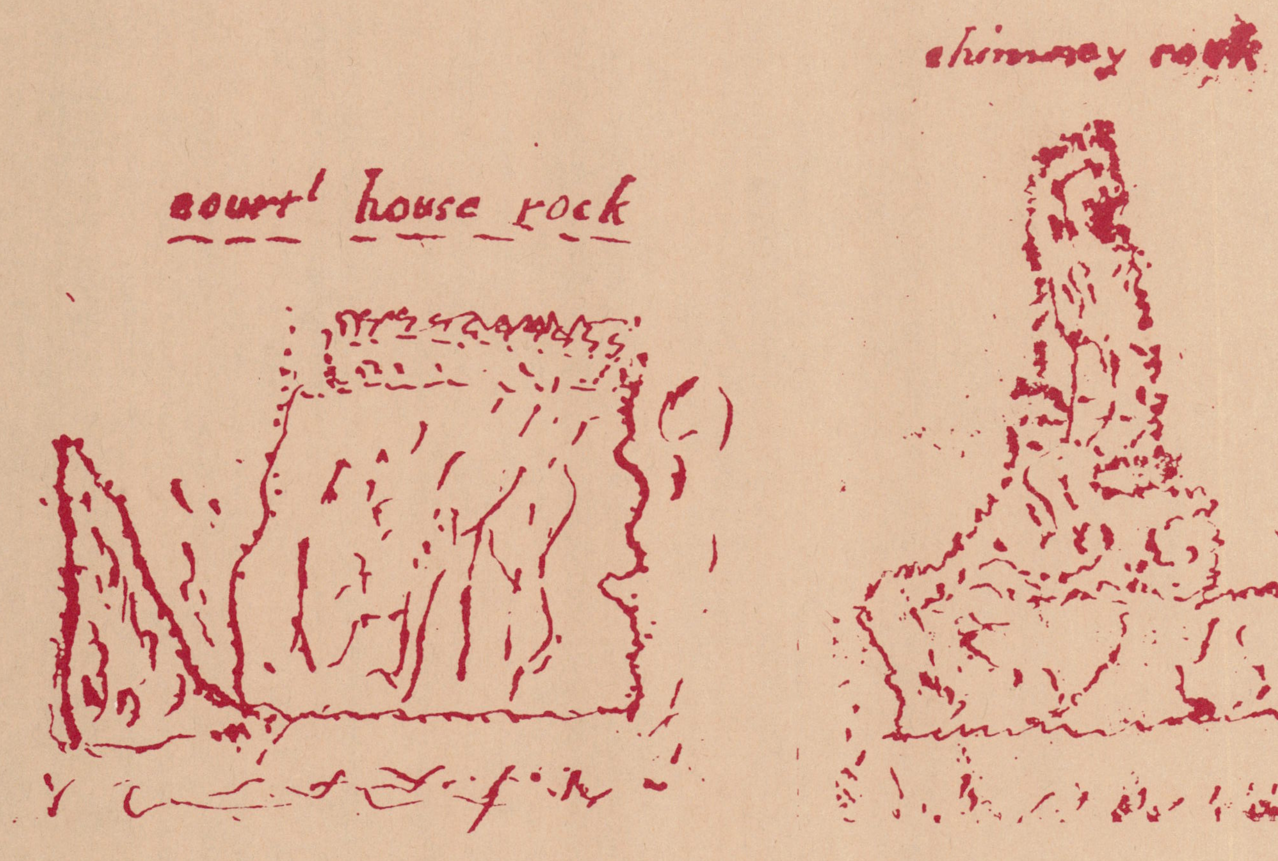

court' house rock
chimney rock

June 9th. Sunday Mor'g. 6 miles west Scotts Bluff. 6 miles further to fine stream clear water; good to camp for 2 miles. Next 7 miles hilly and much heavy sand until strike R(iver) bottom. Water & grass for 3 miles to gravel point of hills & some timber. 2 miles to Trading post. Road on b(an)k River, 15 miles on bottom; grass, wood & water. Road leave River, take(s) hill 5 m. across to Larame Fork. Grass. 1½ m. to Fort. Not allowed to graze near it. Fort situated on Larame Fork, 1½ m. up. Vary pirty situation on W. of river. I did not get within 6 miles of Fort this day. Encamp'd with train from Caliway Co., Mo. Eat the last provisions I had. In good health. Traveled about 38 miles this day. Dr. Richard Jones in my Co.

June 10th. Monday. Rode 6 miles to Fort Larame; arrived at 7 A.M. crowded hard, & got our Breakfast at 37½c each. Registered my name and went back on road 3 miles to graze horses. It hailed in the evening smartly. There is a vast quantity of waggons left here. Traders pretend to trade for them, but pay nothing. I can buy of them a new waggon of choice for $25. Saw a waggon & 4 set harness cost in States $180, given for 4 pack saddles. They sell here at $2 a piece. Returned to Fort at night & got supper & lodging in mess room. Bot to day 2 lb. coffee, 70c; 2 lb. sugar, 60c; 8 lb. Bacon 90c & 5 lb hard Bread, 50c. Wm Bradshaw & Co. passed to day, also Mc Pike & Straughter.[1] See Dr. Bartlett. Buckhamon & Co. arv'd in eve'g, left next day.

June 11th. Tuesday. Left Fort; could get no breakfast. Went back to ford and cooked some provisions and then went 1½ m east to graze horse. Meeker, Fisher, Hawkins, Young & Others of Lewis & Knox Co., Mo. in camp all day washing up on east side Larame Fork on bank. Mc Pike & Co. 3 m. west laying up. See 1 pirty fight at Ford to day with two men in waggon mess. The 3rd man wanted to make peace, and Smith, one of the 1st, made for his arms. After getting a pistol his antagonist disarmed him and did not use the weapon; but Smith made them run their vary best to get out of his way. The 3rd man he made up with & went on; the other

1   This train was the subject of much advance publicity in the newspapers of the day. It was an "Express Passenger Train," and was expected to make the quickest trip of the season. On May 26th, however, it was struck by a tornado and lost 25 of its best horses and mules in the resulting stampede. See Sawyer's Journal, p. 26.

started to the Fort to have the matter settled by Com'd'g officer. I heard no further from them.

June 12th, 13th & 14th. Wednesday, Thursday, & Friday. Remained at crossing of Laremie Ford in camp with Mr. Macalf, a Mountaineer trader waiting for Teem. 13th. Jo Porter, Wm. Marshell, R. Myers & Co., passed. 14th. Jerome Hanson & Smith's Passenger train passed, also Wiles & Bennetts, the Georgia train on the 13th. See Woolery & Stamp. On the 14th, nothing of any important. I buy me bread and meet of the emegrants, wach the road, graze me horse & cook and eat; and am in good health to do all. There is a great sacrifice of waggons at this point in exchanging & cutting up[2] and many burn them for fear they will do others good. 12th. Man drown on N. Platte here crossing.

June 15th. Saturday. Dr. Revely pass'd Laramie Fort in morning. Bournes, Givens, Brown & others of Lewis Co. Mo. 12 Ock same day, Longmyer, Jarvis, Van Noy, Gilbert & Brinentines. Wm Fore & other, evening, of Palmyra & New London, Mo. Mr. A. Church with word from J.H. Frush to me this day at noon; St. Clair with teem & stock same time. U.S. Train and eskort arrived at Fort this evening.

June 16th. Sunday. Still campt'd with Mr. Medcalf on bank of Platte. Grazed east of river in forenoon and tied out in the limits of fort bounds at night. Had a fine mess of Fish for supper with Mr. Medcalf. River vary deep fording. Two deaths reported to day at Forks of River here by Diorear or Colera.

June 17th. Monday. Hall & Elexanders passenger train passed this morning 8 Ock. Estall, same time. Lowdermacks teem & Co., also Van Camp, Hollingsworth & Morse from Bee Town, Wis., crossed, 9 Ock. Man died on E. bank of River at Ford this morning. Croines Drove, of Pike Co., Mo., crossed this day.

2   After leaving Fort Laramie the difficulties of the route increased. As a consequence, it was the custom of the emigrants to here shorten their wagons by cutting off the reaches and wagon boxes, or to purchase or trade their heavy wagons for lighter ones.

June 18th. Tuesday, At noon, John H. Frush, Geo. Griffith & Wm. & Al. Towson crossed Laramie Fork, when I took up with them and passed on 6 miles west of Fort and Encampted in Co. with the Horse shoe Train. Left at Ford in camp with Mr. Medcalf, Kit Carson, the celebrated Rocky Mt. Guide.[3] His advice to me was to go by way of Oregon to California, as the imence Emigration ahead would destroy all the grass on St. Mareys.[4] Boys all well. No. of men up (to) to day passed this Fort, 30964; women, 439; children, 508; waggons, 7113; Horses, 19,886; Mules, 6,470; Oxen, 18, 238; Cows, 2,758.[5]

June 19th. Wednesday. Rode back to Fort, 6 miles. Rote letter to wife; paid 50c to have it carried back to States by Estells Express Mail. Left fort 9 Ock and overtook teems near warm springs west of Fort on upper road 14 miles out. Road good this far—noon. Drove over some hilly road but good to camp at. Creek & springs from Warm Springs 10 miles. Plenty water, grass & Timber there for 10 miles. I was vary unwell with pain over eyes to day & lay up in waggon from noon to night. Camp on Dead timber creek, 1st crossing. Travel about 16 miles past day.

June 20th. Thursday. Alls Well. Follow up fine creek clear water, 10 ft wide x 3, several times for 6 miles. Plenty timber & grass. R(oad) leaves creek & follows dry revene for miles. Grass & timber 6 miles from last creek. 7¾ miles as per Mo(rmo)n Gide[6] from last creek, good spring; no

3   Kit Carson had arrived at the Fort about the first of June with a drove of horses and mules to trade with the emigrants. In his Narrative, as edited by Grant, p. 97, he says he "remained at the Fort for about a month, and disposed of the animals to good advantage."

4   The Humboldt River. Improperly but permanently so named by Fremont in 1845. It will be noted that Carson still adheres to the earlier appelation.

5   A comparison of these figures with those of a somewhat earlier date which are a matter of record, afford an opportunity of definitely gauging the extent and momentum of the emigration. The earlier record—15 days prior to that of the present journalist—is contained in the *Frontier Guardian*, Vol. Two, No. 12. It reads: "From the Plains.—Men, women, children, etc. who had passed Fort Laramie prior to the 3d of June: 11,433 men, 119 women, 99 children, 3188 wagons, 10,900 horses, 3588 mules, 3248 oxen and 233 cows."

6   Evidently Clayton's Latter-Day Saint's Guide, St. Louis, 1848.

water for animals. 5½ miles further Hebers Spring & Horse Creek, a fine bold and rapid stream, 10 ft. wide, 1 ft. deep; vary large spring. Plenty grass & wood. We camp'd here for the night. 2 miles from last spring vary hilly but good road. Last 3½ miles down deep dry sandy hollow; much pine nots over surface of ground. Alls well. 2 foot men stay with us that left St. Joseph when I left. Weather clear & fine.

June 21st. Friday. Struck camp erly. 2½ miles to foot steep hill; plenty water, grass & timber to it. Turn up Spring branch to assend hill ¾ mile up. Several vary steep places; vary hard gravel. 1½ miles to grave left of road. Remains of Wm. Reynolds, died June 19th '50, 21 y(ears) age. ½ mile east & dry branch. Thare was 1 grave on bank of Horse Creek near Heber Spring. From summit of hill, fine view Laramie Peak and surrounding cuntry. Cuntry vary hilly and few distant groves and lone Pines. 5 small creeks in 5 miles; 5th one a spring left of road, the others dry. Plenty wood on all; short & bad grass on them. Vary crooked & hilly roads to Labont River, 8¼ miles. The North road up Platte come in 3 mile east La Bonte River. On this R. camp east side, 1½ miles below Ford. Travel to day 19 miles. All well.

June 22nd. Saturday. Left camp. 5 miles to Branch of La Bonete River. Vary little water, no grass 1 mile before & 4½ after. Drove over red sandy oker land. 2 miles further small creek, dry at crossing. Drove to spring ½ mile below and noon'd by the grave of Mrs. Cook of Ray Co., Mo. By her grave lay her bed and pillow—the last, I got. Her husband died before her on the road at Horse Creek & Heber Spring. ¼ M(ile) W(est) rem(ain)s Sol'n Dill, St. Joseph, Mo. Died June 20th. Lady buried left of Road to day 2 m further west. 6¾ miles vary small creek, little water & grass. 1½ m. to La Prela R. Campt 1 m. below ford on west side of river. Fine grass, wood & water. ½ mile east of ford, on top of hill n(orth) of Road 50 yards, the grave of Alex. Best (of) Ills. Died 20th June. Our mess & Co. of 2 waggons all well. Some slight sickness in our train—the Horse Shoe—of 9 waggons. Travel to day 19 miles.

June 23rd. Sunday. Lay over all day in camp to rest our animals. Fine grass and they fared well. We aired our goods, done some washing & sleeping and lighting of loose plunder out of waggons. Enjoyed ourselves well & live in expectation of making a move on to morrow. Not much travel on route

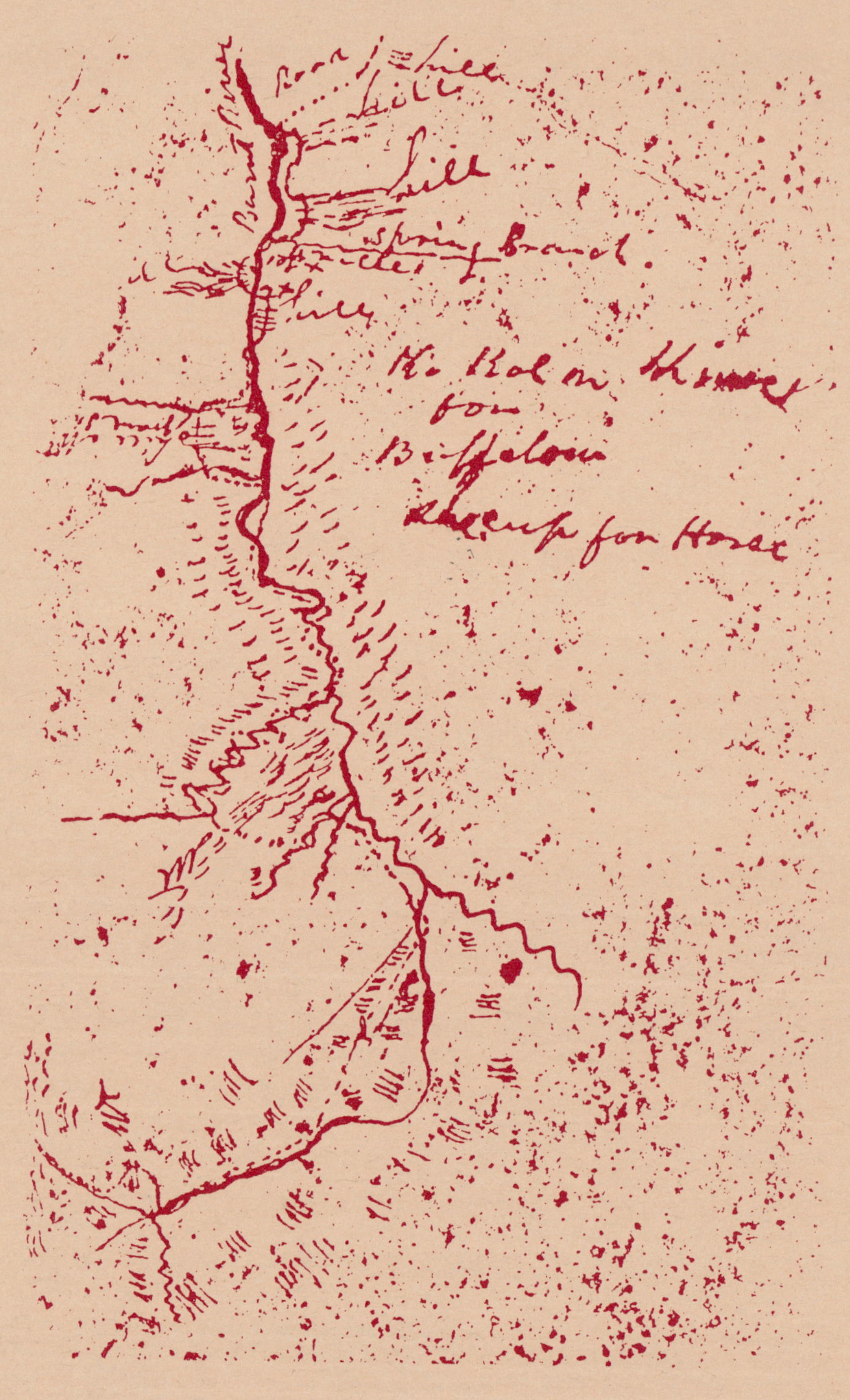

spring branch

to day. Many laying by on this creek to day. 3 men in Train sick with Diorear, but not considered ill. Our Co. all well. The road from here to Platte is good—some hilly—and thin & short grass.

June 24th. Monday. Left camp in good order. 4¼ m to small creek; little water & clear. 1 mile, Box Elder Creek; 5 ft wide, vary clear & fine. Bad crossing. 3¼ m Fourche Boise R. 30 ft wide, 2 deep. Grass & wood. N. Fork Platte River, 4 miles. No grass. 5 miles to Deer Creek. Sandy road, fine stream 30 ft wide, 2 deep. Grass & timber, if not on road, up it. A cole bank up it ¼ mile from road. A Fary on Platte at this point. Was offered a waggon box for Ferry at this place for $50. Campt 3 miles up Deer Creek on good grass & wood. 3 men yet sick. Passed the grave of Sarah C. Brown, Polk Co., Mo., ¼ mile west Prele River, N(orth of) road. 4 miles N. & East ¼ m. of small branch on right road, Jno. N. Cotton, Pike Co., Ill. Died June 20th; also Jno. Putnam, of Henry Co., Mo., died June 23rd. Grave 60 yds west Fouche Boise River, on bank N. road. Travel to day 18 miles. Emigrants on the R(iver) cut(tin)g up waggons to pack.

June 25th. Tuesday. Left camp 3 m. up Deer Creek and kept up creek 3 miles, then turned to right & took up Mt—good road—and decended in main road at deep ravene 8¼ miles from its crossing Deer Creek. Plenty grass on this route. To get this, turn off 1½ m. east Deer Creek to left for 6 miles from camp. 1 m. to grove timber on Platte. 1 mile to Crooked Muddy and vary steep banks. No water, no grass nor wood. 5¾ m. to Muddy Creek. 1¾ m. East took to left of road toward Mt for good grass. Had good grass 1 mile off Road. John H. Frush killed 1 antelope & 3 Mt Rabits to day; we devided in Train and all had a fine Sup'r. Our sick mending. All going on well. We are now on the Platte and 12 miles below Up(per) Ferry. Thare is a Ferry 8 miles above this camp at 2 revenes 4 miles below Up. Ferry, but it is a poor facility. Travel to day 20 miles.

June 26th. Wednesday. Travel'd to Up'r Ferry[7] by 12 Ock A.M. Had no delay. 5 boats in order with ropes and pulley. Crossed train 9 waggons in 1½ hours. Price $5 per waggon; $1 per head for cattle; 50c horses & mules. Drove stock 2 miles up River and swam them at Sand bar in river. Good place. All safe & little trouble. Haul'd out 3 m. and campt 2 m. to

7   The site of present-day Casper, Wyoming.

left of road. Had a suff't of grass. No wood nor water. Wild Sage plenty. Travel to day 15 miles.

June 27th. Thursday. Left camp & traveled 19 miles to Alkili Springs beyond Rock Ave and grazed. Cattle kept from water. The(n) drove to Willow Springs & Correlled cattle all night, as no grass to be had. Thare is another of those Springs 9 m. east of the above, but the one near Willow Springs is a Valley full of them. They are highest in center and like a bason of morter. Many cattle mire and are lost in them. The ground in 3 valleys & revenes is around them covered 1 in deep and places more with a white salt. The Mtns near are white with it. The road near is strew'd with dead stock in the neigh'ood of these springs. All well. Travel cunt(r)y all burnt up; no vegitation. 23 miles travel to day.

June 28th. Friday. Left Willow Springs day light and travel 6¼ miles to fine B(ranch) of water 300 yds S. of road. Fish in it, & drove cattle 4 m. s(outh) to good grass. Grass on Creek all eat off. Desert sand & sage on all the hills & hollows off water courses. Boys Kill'd a No. of Prarie Squrles here. Near is the grave of Dall Capps, Pike Co., Ills. Died the 27th. Grazed until 2 Ock and drove on within 4 miles of Independants Rock near Alkili swamps & campt in bason west of road. Sorounded with Alkili springs. Herded cattle in bason on good grass whare there was no Alkili. This is the place the M(ormon) Gide directs you to get you Saleratis.[8] Thare is a number of Lakes here with a white salt on them vary near 1 in. Thick. Travel to day 16½ miles. All well.

June 29th. Saturday. Struck out from camp day light. Crossed Sweetwater at Independant Rock whare we first struck it. Nooned 4 m. S(outh) near Mtn on left of road, and passed Devile Gate in Evening & campt 7½ miles above on Sweet water. Fine grass here.

June 30th. Sunday. In camp of 29th laying over. Visited the highest peak north of camp & 2nd to any of Sweet water Mts. Wrote a letter to Mrs. A.E. Frush on the summit; built also a fire on it. Jno. H. Frush, Geo. Griffith & Shaw in Co. with me. We had a vary romantic view of the Rocky

8   This seems to confirm the view that Frush was traveling by Clayton's Guide; Clayton here saying: "Here gather your Saleraetus from a lake west of the road."

dome topt rock   pure granite
25 miles wast devils gate, the same from
Independe
nce rock

Mts. West covered with snow; some drifts on Mts south. Height above streem 2000 (ft). This was one of the most butifull views I have ever seen. These Mts are detached ranges and valleys, and of solid granite rock; no earth on them, and are worthy a travelers time to visit them. We had frost this morning.

July 1st. Monday. Quit camp all well. Thare is a vary pirty bottom on this River from Devils Gate up for 10 miles, 1½ miles wide affords fine grass. It then gets narrow, not more than ½ mile to whare road runs through mtn about 28 miles from Devils Gate. For particulars of road see Mormon Guide. The table on bason lands between Mts produce nothing but sand & wild sage. This table or valley is 6 to 10 miles wide on the north side the Sweet Water Mts, with each hill its valley, and of smooth solid granite. South a continued range of Mts. with its sides covered with pine & many places snow drifts make appearance. I have not traveled one day for the last 10 that I did not find a number of waggons cut up and many burn by Emigrants in fitting and abandoning them to pack. 25 m. from Devils Gate is the Doom Top Mt north of road. Solid granite & not a deface or ruff formation on it—as clean as the rain of time could wash it. Waggons campt 6½ m. East of 2nd crossing of this River. I went forward to (next) crossing; J(ohn) and teems not coming on. Stay with a company from Johnston Co., Mo. The road for 8 miles to here is vary sandy & heavy. Teems travel to day about 15 miles & all well.

July 2nd. Tuesday. Travel to day about 15 miles to 4th crossing on Sweet Water, but kept on South Side all day, and the whole road heavy sand. The ford at 3rd crossing being bad, we kept the old road which is a sand desert with a little wild sage on it. Passed Baldwin, of Shelby Co., Mo., at 2nd crossing S(weet) W(ater). Many cattle was left here by getting wore out. I see six this morning and heard of several more. Nearly every camp place you still find a distruction of waggons. We are this evening in full view of the Mts west which a(re) white with snow. We are now at the foot of one of the Sweet Water Mts—still a clean pile of Granite Rock. I have bin on two to day, to cut out of the crevices two bundles of grass with my butcher knife to feed my horse. The grass in bottom is vary vary short.

July 3rd. Wednesday. Traveled to day 17 miles & campt on Sweetwater at Ford No. 6. This day I was taken with a fever and severe pains in my limbs with shortness of breath as if produced by the want of proper atmosphere pressure. I suffered much and took medicine in the night. Our road to day was a heavy sandy one. No grass; sand & wild sage plenty.

July 4th. Thursday. Lay up all day. Myself & Hobbs being sick. We boat(h) improved by delay. Found feed 1½ miles off Road & stock done well.

July 5th. Friday. Travel to day 18 miles over vary rocky & hilly road, and raised to high Elevation — barren. Campt on branch of Sweet Water 18 m. East of S(outh) Pass. I lay all day in waggon, not able to walk, or ride my horse. This camp was at snow drift on creek 6 ft deep.

July 6th Saturday. Traveled 15 m. to day and camp 3 mile of summitt of S. Pass, East side. I rode horse back all day. Felt vary much worried at night. This South pass or gap in the Mtn here is a body of table land rolling but not mountainous, 15 miles wide. The Mts are white with snow 10 miles north of us. Plenty deep drifts in sight & on road side all day, 5 to 8 ft deep.

July 7th. Sunday. Finished my letters that I com(mence)d on Sweet Water Mt. last evening. This morning we traveled to Pacific Spring. John & I sent out letters by J.M. Estiles Ex. Mail; paid 50c each. We traveled on this day to Little Sandy and herded at river all night. Distance traveled to day 26 miles.

From Sweet Water to South Pass	10 miles
To Pacifc Spring	3 miles
To Creek Crossing	1½ miles
Dry Sandy (& Bad water)	9 miles
To Forks of road — Sublett's Cut off	6 miles
To Little Sandy. 2 r(ods) wide, 2 ft deep	4 miles
To Big Sandy. 4 R. wide; 2 ft Deep	5 miles
To Green River	45 miles

This entire road from Pacific Spring is a vary level Sandy and Ashy desert. No grass on the streams. The Sands and ashes drift like snow. Thare is 3 deep revenes near Green River, 8, 6, & 4 miles from River & steep hill at river. This is the place to try men & cattle. It is one level flat across and to what extent N. & South I do not no. No Mountains as you might suppose.

July 8th. Monday. We traveled from Little Sandy 5 miles to Big Sandy & turned out our cattle 7 miles up river, with a number of men to herd them. Here we lay the 9th, & left 10th at noon. I was here again vary unwell while here, by exposing myself to(o) soon.

July 11th. Thursday. After driving all night we made Green River at 12 Ock M, on this day. Crossed and swam our stock & drove 5 miles up river to a Prong of it and camp'd.

> Paid for Ferry of Waggon $7.00
> Paid for Ferry of Horse . . . . $1.50 a head
> Paid for Ferry of Oxen . . . . $2.00 a head

Geo. had two ferried of his, the ballance swam. This day I go about again. Thare is much Alkili water near the Ferry on boath sides and a vary large number of dead stock about it. Stream 100 yds wide, vary swift & deep—dangerous to cross. Boats & facilities good; business disposed in order.

July 12th. Friday. We lay buy all day & discharged our waggon into Griffiths, to leave one and splice teems. Geo. is vary sick to day; fever & much pain. Taken last night. The vally on bottom on this river is a poor burnt up ash and sand bottom; produces but little grass—that, only whare the ground is wet, and the whole surrounded by high steep hills or mountains of sand. It is not fit for anything. It has bin vary much misrepresented. I heard that it was a rich valley. It is not the fact. It is a miserable valley; but good water. Thare is many Emigrants laying here to day recruiting. Thare was many took the Salt Lake Road after crossing Green River, by going down west side after strikeing one of its branches 8 miles below the Ferry.

July 13th. Saturday. Left camp & passed down by Ferry. From Upper Ferry to Branch of Green River, 2 rods wide, 2 ft deep, 8 miles. Vary crooked & vary steep—hilly road & heavy sand and ashes; vary dusty. We nooned here. Left one waggon belonging to Horse Shoe Co. We traveled up this creek bottom 6 miles before we leave it. Good road & fine grass—the best for 100 miles. We camp'd whare road leaves, and done well. Griffith is getting well. Left Baldwin on this Creek at noon herding his cattle. He leaves tomorrow to travel on after.

July 14th. Sunday. Left one of Co. waggons this morning and travel on 4 miles to vary small spring branch; 4 miles further do; 2 miles do to Fur Wood grove and Springs. All the road vary crooked & hilly; deep ashes. 4 miles to small spring branch at foot of the 2nd vary steep hill. Thare is two hills here to decend; vary steep, ½ mile long. Plenty snow drifts at Fur Wood Springs. Nooned here. ½ mile good spring. Water for 2 miles. 1 mile further, fine creek, 4 ft wide 1 ft deep. Last 3 miles good road. Many strati rock ridges. No dust; and grass on ridges. A spring branch every mile for next 4 miles. Here we campt. Travel to day 21 miles.

July 15. Monday. Geo. Griffith lost 1 Stier this morning. McChristy also one. We traveled 5 miles further to Hams Fork of Green River, 4 rods wide, 2 ft deep and campt for the day. Here the Co. lost 3 more stiers. This is a fine valley of grass; the best we have had for 200 miles. Mostly *red top*. Thare is a large number of the Snake Indians campt here. We campt with them. They are inteligent & civil, and have a large quantity of fine horses. Thare is a vary steep mountain to assend and decend 5 miles before you get to this river. Thare is a road at the foot of it on the East side; if followd down the mountain to the left (this road) will shun it (the steep mtn), and only increase the distance 3 miles. We had a vary fine mess of Speckled Trout for supper, which is plentiful in River. No timber but willows on River. Some Aspen groves on side of the mountain and some snow drifts. We had a heavy frost in the night; wet clothes froze stiff and ice made in water that set in bucket.

July 16th. Tuesday. 6 miles to fine spring left (of) road. First 1½ miles a vary steep mountain, then to spring good road. 5 miles to fine spring branch. Long hilly & crooked mountain to assend and the same vary steep to decend to it from here. 2 miles to summit another mountain crooked & steep, & 1½ miles to decend, also vary steep & rough. 6 miles from foot to Bear River. Road good. We fixed camp right road next Mt., 2 miles from foot. Fine grass & good spring at Mt. John Frush & myself reconnortered same of the pine thickets south of the Road. 11 miles from Hams Fork thare is quite a cannon in the valley and vary heavy & think pine & Fur wood timber on north side of Mt., south of revene or cannon. Much timber was here broken down by heavy snow drifts. John found an oxen and drove him on our tramp. The road does not run to river, but is 1½ miles east on bottom. This is whare the old Fort Bridger Road come down the River. This River Runs north here.

July 17th. Wednesday. We traviled from within 2 miles of foot of mountain up Bear River bottom to large Fork putting in from east side, 4 rods wide 2 ft deep—Thomas Fork. Distance from foot of Mountain 10 miles. Here we drove 1½ miles up *East Fork* Thomas Fork and campt until next day. Bear River here affords a fine bottom from 1 to 5 miles wide and most exelent grass. No wood but some willow on banks of River & Creeks. Thare is a vary high mountain on each side and narrow gap whare East fork comes in. The road is vary obstructed at crossing by the river being cut up by 4 differant shoots of the river. Thare is a vary rough piece of road for ½ mile after crossing the river, caused by heavy rocks which has dropt from Mt above. From here to north bend of River, about 15 miles, a vary level & fine road down River bottom; much good grass and a number of Springs running across the road from the Mountain. We had another fine mess of Trout for supper & one for breakfast.

July 18th. Thursday. We traveled to day down River to North Bend, or Muddy Fork and campt on East side of River bottom next to the mountain, on a vary large rapid spring creek, 6 ft wide 1 ft deep. Plenty of grass and willow for wood. John left the ox he found on road; he could not travel. Distance from last camp on Prong of river as stated yesterday, about 15 miles, which is from Thomas Fork to Muddy Fork. Muddy Fork 4 rods wide, 2 ft deep.

July 19th. Friday. Muddy Fork to foot of mtn., 1½ miles; 1 do to Top. Good spring half way up, left (of) road. 1½ miles to Branch in valley. Fine grass on it; no wood. 1 mile to Branch, 4 ft wide, in same valley. ½ mile to ft. Mt.; 1½ miles to top—vary steep. ½ mile down revene. Then up gap and gradual assend for 1½ miles to summit. 1 mile down vary steep Mt to Bear River bottom again. Total distance across point Mt., from Muddy Fork to this point, 10 miles. Crossing this point of Mtn is to avoid a bend in River south. 8 miles to branch crossing road, 10 ft wide, 1 ft deep. Vary good road down River bottom; grass in abundance. Bottom at crossing of this Branch, 3 miles wide. Plenty of Trout in it. We campt on this Branch east (of) road. All well. We traveled 20 miles to day. Plenty of snow drifts on top of Mt near us. Vary warm in valley during day—nights cool.

July 20th. Saturday. To fine Spring branch 3 ft wide, 6 in deep, 4½ miles. No wood at crossing. Some willows on it. To fine Spring Branch, 6 ft wide, 6 in deep, ½ mile. Some willow on it. To another, 3 ft wide, 6 in. deep, ½ mile, some willow on it; plenty up the next mt. Fine Branch Spring, ¾ mile, 2 ft wide, 6 in deep. Fine do, 3 ft wide, 6 in deep, 2½ miles. do do, 2 miles. 2 fine Rivers, 1 mile further—near together, between them, ¼ mile. At them, Snake Indian Encampment. These creeks are 6 ft wide, 10 in deep, and vary rapid. 3 miles to spring & branch. Road here leaves River & passes through gap & point (of) Mt, 2 miles to revene leading to left down to river. Here we drove down & campt. Distance 1½ miles. Fine grass & wood. Plenty of wild currents here and plenty of snow drifts on Mt top south 3 miles. Traveled on road to day 17 miles. Plenty of water & wood & grass in this pass.

July 21st. Sunday. We lay in camp until 3 Ock P.M., to day. From pass & revene leading to River to the grave of Melkiah Everman of Knox Co., Mo., 2 miles. Died 5th July, '50, and is buried on right of road, 10 rods, and 11 miles this side of Soda Springs. 2 miles to small spring, right road. Aspen grove on left. 1½ miles to good spring, left road. Road good from Indian camp to this spring, but rolling. We campt at Springs, 1 mile left road; here there is many of them. Had Indians to Eat with us night & morning.

July 22nd. Monday. From fine springs, left road to branch 2 ft wide, 7 miles. To Creek 20 ft wide, 6 in deep and Soda Springs, 1½ (miles). Steam Boat Springs, or last of Soda Springs on road, 1 mile. Thare is quite a Ceder grove here in neighborhood of these springs. Thare is a number of Indian Lodges here trading. This water tastes like Soda or Beer, and boils with much rapidity out of the earth. Thare is a number of them on this mile of road—all near the bank of Bear River, a stream here 50 yds wide. Thare is much appearance of Boiling Springs and volcanic eruptions in this country. Thare is much yellow oaker formed by the boiling of these springs that are least pregnated with soda. 4 miles beyond this the road forks—the Right to Fort Hall, the left, Hudspeths cut off. 5 mile on right hand road, good spring right (of) road. Here we campt. Thare is good grass and good road the days travel. Thare is much appearance of volcanic

Eruptions for the last 5 miles. Thare is fine & wide valley on left & fine grass. This valley is from 7 to 8 miles wide. For the next 15 miles you pass up it on the East side, a fine road. The valley has the appearance all the way of former Volcano, as is evident from the quantity of black cave rock and hollow ovens or piles of it in every direction. Thare is a high range of Mts on boath sides. Snow plenty on the west view of Mt.

July 23rd. Tuesday. ½ mile to fine spring on left of road—tastes a little sour. 9½ miles to fine branch, 6 ft wide, 1 ft deep, also a little sour, but I think good to use, No wood; some willow 1½ miles up to right. 2 miles to creek 10 ft wide, 18 in deep; no wood at crossing—1 mile up it, plenty willow. We went up this, 1 mile & campt on road after crossing branch. 9½ miles from Spring we left the volcanic appearance of Eruptions on the road & fall on to a leveler bottom of fine grass—red top & spear grass—which has much the appearance of blue grass. Thare is plenty of wild rye & Flax. The Flax grows all along on this River [Bear River] from whare we first struck it. The soil here is of a rich & fertile appearance and produces grass equal to any meadow, and the valley here at this camp point is at least 6 miles wide. Green River to East, and west, range of Mts seperating the waters of the great Bason and Columbia Rivers is the Shoshawnia [Shoshone] Indians. North of this Range, the Panaca [Bannack] Indians. The[y] mix and are friendly to Each other and the Whites.

July 24th. Wednesday. 4 miles up Creek to crossing. Here we cross & turn to left & to mouth of hollow bottom, here 1 mile wide and fine grass. Crossing 10 ft wide, 2 ft. deep. 2 miles up left valley to fine spring dreen and Aspen grove. Here we follow up a noch or gap in Mt., and cross 5 fine spring dreans in the next 2½ miles. We then come to steep point to assend & crooked road at point. Thare is no valley in this gap. Road rough & a thicket of Aspen timber for the last 2½ miles, and a fine run of good water to this point of road. 2½ miles from here to summit of Mt. Gradual rise but road rolling over short points. Plenty of wood & grass but no water. 1½ miles from summit to vary large & fine spring left road. We go down this branch, which is the first waters we strike of the Columbia River, or Branch of Lewis River. 1 mile further another large spring, 30 ft diameter 4 ft deep; affords a stream 4 ft wide, 1 ft deep on the right of road—200 yards to crossing drean. 1 mile to another fine spring drean. Here we campt. Vary good road down the Mt. on this side; gradual desend, and from 2nd big spring, a valley 2 miles wide. Good grass and Aspen groves next Mt. Many snow drifts on Mt west of road & ¾ mile off; and fine pine woods on same. This is between two last drains on Mt. Mountains on each side high, but smooth surface—clear of rock; many broken points. Travel to day 14 miles.

July 25th. Thursday. 1 mile further to fine spring branch. 1 do do to fine do. 1 mile steep hill to desend to main run down the valley. Here the Mt form a Kanyon or gap leaving road narrow space to pass. This run here at crossing is 8 ft wide 2 ft deep made by the springs & dreans above discents. We do not pass through this Kanyon, but pass on side of Mt with gradual desend to run again. Distance to avoid it, and where we strike run from first crossing, 1 mile. This is a vary romantic place and much rocky precipices on each side & ceder timber that [is] scrubby. Here we strike a large valley of roaling cuntry. North of this [is the] east & west range of Mts which seperate the great bason from the Columbia. We keep down this run on creek for 6 miles to foot of hill whare creek leaves road. Plenty willow and wild oats & Rye on it. Good road. 1 mile creek returns to road & road follows down on right of creek; on & near it for 5 miles. Here we campt. After traveling 3 miles from whare creek returned to road you strike a level bottom tending down from the north, which gives us here a fine view of the three Mound Mountains or 3 Tentons which is situated northward; the first about 20 the second 30 and the third 30 miles off. This is a vary wide level valley; the 2nd bottom deep black sand. Fort Lorin[9] is on a creek comeing from the north down the valley. Thare is many vary large springs through this bottom that make grate runs from them.

July 26th. Friday. From whare road bears to right & leaves the Creek—it is here ¾ mile south—to crossing of Creek comeing from north, 6 miles. Creek 20 ft wide, 1 ft deep. Vary heavy sand for 8 miles. 1 mile to opposite fort Lorin; cross 3 springs in this mile; plenty grass, willow & water. To Fort Hall 5 miles. Crossed another creek, 20 ft wide, 1 ft deep in next mile. Road for 6 miles to Fort Hall runs on bottom, and 6 miles from Fort Hall also runs on bottom. This is one of the finest natural meadows I ever saw. Fort Hall is situated on the south bank of Snake or Lewis River, and is an

9   Fort Loring, or more properly Cantonment Loring.

Emmence bottom; but with vary little cotton wood timber on the River only. This is a post built and belongs to the Hudson Bay Co. Fort Lorin, 5 miles up Snake River is an American post. Thare is an American Co., trading at the latter post, Owens,[10] Rich & Co., and at Fort Hall is a Co., belonging to the Hudson Bay Co., who pack all their supplies from Fort Vancouver. Thare is a number of Indians with them at Fort. That had a large & vary Extra number of Horses. 4 miles from Fort Hall to crossing of Creek, 60 ft wide, 2 ft deep; pure spring water, and made from the large springs crossed to day. On the bank of this we campt for the night. Travel to day 16 miles. Distance given at Fort Hall 40 miles to fork of the California Road; 300 miles to Fort Boise; 500 miles to Blue Mt.; 700 miles to Dalls.

July 27th. Saturday. From crossing Creek to Fentneuf [Port Neuf] River crossing, 2 miles. This River is 75 yards wide, 3 ft deep. You rise immediately from crossing of River up steep hill 100 yards Long to second bottom. You travel then on dry, level ridge for 8 miles to crossing of another creek 10 ft wide, 2 ft deep and vary muddy & myere to cross. No bottom of any size on it. You then travel up to similar bench to the last 8 miles travel, and travel on it for 6 miles to fine spring whare road strikes bottom. This dry second bottom has but little grass and plenty wild sage. You follow it on the Edge of 1st bottom, and can camp at any place on road by driving your stock ½ mile to River Bottom, as far as within 1 mile of the Am[erica]n Falls, which is from spring, 5 miles. 5 miles from spring 1 mile below, is a steep hill to desend & Assend crossing revene — but short. 3 miles, road run[s] to river bank. Steep hill to desend; good place to water stock. ½ mile steep hill to assend to bench. Short 1½ miles to Fall Creek, 6 ft wide, 1 ft deep. 1 mile to small branch, 3 ft wide, 6 in deep. ½ mile to Steep rock point on right of road, & head of rapids in River. Here the River is closed in on boath sides by a high precipice of perpindicular rock, which make it narrow. Thare is two deep revenes to cross in the next ½ mile, which is steep going in & out. The road down this river in the distances given above is generally level. On the bench of second bottom thare is no River bottom to afford grass after you get to 1 mile of the Amer. Falls until you get to the head of rapids. To Rock Aviniew, 3½ miles.

10 Major John Owen. See the Journal & Letters of Major John Owen, N.Y., 1927, Vol. 1, p. 227. Therein it is recorded that C.W. Frush was the Major's Commissary during the late fifties.

½ mile to [where] road strikes River, good watering place—no camp.
½ mile to vary rapid & rocky creek 8 ft wide, 1 ft deep. Had to cross ½ mile
to River again. Good to camp.

July 28th. Sunday. Visited the American Falls of Lewis River. They have a
perpendicular Fall in 300 yds of about 60 ft, and are about 250 yards wide.
Caused by a heavy chain of volcanic Rock extending across. Thare is every
appearance of fire being one time here, from cinders & glass formed by
melting of sand & Flint. This is a vary romantic place; the falls are [a]
connected sheet of water across the river. Cross section of them thus;
[Sketch of falls in Ms]. The perpendicular at foot is about 20 ft; the rest
above, and incline plane. The river is vary slow current above and
immediately below. I also visited the narrows & rapids 7½ miles below.
The perpindicular here is not more than 4 or five ft; direct, not over 2 ft.
½ mile below this is Rock Island, about 500 yds long & 100 yds wide;
rounding on each side to Top and about 60 ft high. 3½ miles to Rock
Avinieu or gateway. This is a narrow passage, very level, passing through a
high range of Rocks, vary black, that is thrown across a bason or level
bottom between River & Mt. Thare is still no bottom on the River, but 2 or
[3] dry bench. The last 3½ miles if vary hilley, also the next 1½ miles, but
thare is a good camp place in the next 1½ miles. Here we campt for this
night. The river from the Falls this far and continuous, is closed in by
perpendicular cliffs of black promitive Rock which cuts off the lowe
bottom from the Mtn falls.

July 29th. Monday. From River ½ mile down from rocky branch to
crossing of Fall River, 3 miles. River 15 ft wide, 2 ft deep. 3 miles from
whare road leaves River, good place to camp here and at cross[in]g of Fall
River. Good Road—steep to crossing of River. Road here leaves Lewis
River for 30 miles. Long gradual hills to assend and decend to Raft River.
Distance 5 miles, good road & plenty of grass and wild sage; no water until
Raft River—here plenty grass, water & Willow. River 20 ft wide, 2 ft deep.
Water cloudy. At this place the Oregon Road takes to right; the California
up Fall River. Here we campt for the day. Travel to day on road 11 miles.
John had ox to die at this River.

July 30th. Tuesday. From Raft River to next water, 15 miles. Road
generally level, but many round, loose rock in it that makes it rough to

drive over, and has been a vast volcanic cuntry from appearance of rock, which is a black Lava. Plenty sage & grass on road. The first water is a cat-tail swamp or marsh. 1 mile from whare you strike is a creek—Swamp Creek—12 ft wide, 2 ft deep. Rocky, and fine at this place to water at. Vary bad to water stock at any place below, & for 2 miles whare road leaves it. We campt below 2 miles, whare road leaves creek to left, 2 miles. Travel to day 18 miles. Wide marshes above watering place & no bottom below. Good grass to camp.

July 31st. Wednesday. From whare road leaves creek on left, to whare it strikes it again, 3½ miles. Down creek to whare road crosses, ½ mile. Good place to camp. Last ½ mile, water handy and good grass. Road level & good for last 4 miles. The Big River is within ½ mile of this crossing. J. Frush had a vary fine ox to die here to day. We only drove the last 4 miles & campt for balance of the day on account of some sick stock in the train. Plenty Fish in this creek. No soil nor timber from Am. Falls—burnt rock & Ashes.

August 1st. Thursday. From crossing creek to whare road runs to River, 3 miles; good road. Road runs on low bottom, 1½ miles & leaves bottom; do to camp. Wild Rye & Sage; grass not good. This is the first time the road has run to Lewis R. for 30 miles. Road left River 3 miles below Fall River. 4½ miles to Creek, 15 yds wide, 2 ft deep. Good grass & fine for camp. This is Goose Creek. To whare road nears River bank, 6½ miles. Good & level road, but some dusty. Good place to camp at River. Road runs down River 1 mile to opposite high Rock Island in ce[n]tre River. Vary raged surface, 60 ft high, 300 yards long, 160 wide. 1 mile below is a large regular Elevated Island of oval shape, ½ mile long, with a few pine trees on head of it. Thare is no timber on this River—some willow in places on banks. I will call this last Island, Eagle Island, as thare is a large eagle nest on the head of it. From Eagle Island to Dry Creek, 8½ miles. Some seeder timber on it, but no water. Good place to water stock at mouth this creek. The last 5 miles is vary ruff road; big many loose rock in it. Thare is vary great Rapids in River for 6 miles here and the cliffs on each side high. We travel on bench as usual, above their Elevation. Cuntry generally level. The River narrow'd by the precipices closing; the land unproductive. Black Rock, sage and Ashes, but poor for grass. Snow on Mts to left 7 or 8 miles off. Campt on dry creek. Travel to day 21 miles. Plenty snakes here.

August 2nd. Friday. From Dry Creek to Willow Creek, 7 miles. Coole Spring whare you first strike it under bank. Not much water, only in Pans. 10 miles to next water, fine creek 15 ft wide, 1 ft deep, left road. Good to camp. The road leaves the River in commencing this 10 miles. The River turns North, and is for 6 miles above vary rapid & narrow, and is walled in by perpendicular cliffs; vary high — impossible to approach it. The rock is a vary black tecture. Thare is a vary narrow falls at the mouth of Willow Creek — Creek a little above, say 1 mile. From whare road nears the creek to crossing of the same, 8 miles. The road does not run with creek, but crosses bend. Vary good road. Good place to camp. At crossing here the creek is walled in with narrow bottom 200 yds wide in places, by a steep perpendicular black rock on boath sides, and not accessable to get to with stock for several miles above and below crossing. *Crossing good.* From ford to whare road leaves creek at short deep revene running into creek commencing at right of road and has some Seeder trees growing in bottom of it, 6 miles. This is the only place thare is any Seeder on the creek. Whare road passes thare is good grass on the bottom of the creek, which is from 50 to 200 yds wide, but vary few places to get stock down. From whare road leaves creek to whare road runs to Top of River bluff whare stock can be got down, 8 miles. Thare is a large fall of water caused by spring on opposite side of River at this place. Road good & camp.

August 3rd. Saturday. The distances of to days travel proceeding page. The country round is a vast level plane between Mts which are so distant that you can make but little out of their appearance, and as unproductive country as any we have travel through. It produced this year no grass; plenty small sage. The general character of the appearance of the earth is much that of a mud hole by the road side after it has dried up. Rock Creek is a curiosity. It is a deep crivice or chanel for the creek & Bottom to pass, which looks as if it had been worked down in the solid rock by art, and when you are near it thare is on the surface, no appearance of it. The walls are 50 to 60 ft high. The Main River has the same appearance with its plain walls on each side of 400 ft the distance we see it on to days travel, and in many places approaches the waters edge; in others it will recede back & leave a small bottom — this not frequent. The road, after it leaves rocky creek about 4 miles, forks. The right hand will lead to the camp place on Bluff of river with the convience of driving down bluff to water; the left hand road does not come within a mile of it, but is some nearer.

They come together one mile from the camp ground whare thare is a grave on left at edge of road at their junction. This camp is supposed to be on the ground that Col. Fremont once campt at & discribed in his Travels. Cross section of the River ginerally for last 100 miles: [pen sketch in original Ms.]

August 4th. Sunday. From camp on Bluff the road turns square south and falls into main road, 1 mile. 1 mile further cross Dry revene. Some seeder timber on boath sides in revene at crossing. 1 mile further cross another Dry revene, some seeder down it to right, one lone seeder to left, 200 yds from road. The road here inclines southwest, then west & then south, making from Fremonts camp on Bluff a half circle. It then inclines west; and vary good road. No grass & the first water is whare road Decends river bluff to near river. Not much if any grass. Distance from last revene, 9 miles. This is on a high sandy bottom. The River is narrow here and vary great rapids. On the opposite side is a stream of water that is 30 to 40 ft wide, rushing down a steep fall, 20 or 30 ft into the river. This comes out of a solid bluff on the River that is 300 ft above it. Has the appearance of some river that has sunk and found its outlet here. Thare is no appearance of a stream on the surface. 3 miles from here the road strikes river at the crossing of a small branch, 2 ft wide, 6 in deep. Thare is a good place to water stock at river. The bank is a flat sand bar and will do to camp on as thare is some grass. About 100 yds above the river has a rapid fall of 20 ft in 100 yds, but I do not think thare is half the quantity of water in river here as at the Am. Falls above; it certainly sinks. The road is vary heavy sand for the last 3 miles. Thare is a good place to camp on river one mile below; we campt at it. Bottom narrow, but grass sufficient for small Emigration. Plenty fish here. We enjoyed them. Travel to day 16 miles.

August 5th. Monday. From good place to camp 1 mile down river from branch, the road leaves River & runs to left up valley for 2 miles and strikes a vary fine creek, 50 ft wide, 1 ft deep; you go down this one mile and cross it near its mouth. First rate place to camp at crossing & good places from [where] you first strike it. There is two roads here, one round the river bottom, the other across point, which is steep & broken until you strike river again at Salmon Falls, which is 4 miles. The road round the river is the best but some further & is preferred. We travel the cut off and come together at Falls. These Falls are about 1½ miles long and vary rapid. The perpendicular within 1½ miles must be 60 to 80 ft, but thare is no abrupt fall to exceed 4 to 6 ft. They are about 100 yds wide, and many Islands in them. You can ford the[m]. We drove our stock on one of the[m] to feed & stay from noon to dark; then drove on to the next water, 14½ miles to top of Bluff whare road nears river, & drove stock down—vary steep—one mile to water. No grass at this place; but little at Falls. Vary poor 4 miles above them, and little or none beyond for 20 miles. Thare was a number of the Digger Indians at Salmon Falls fishing. They had bin some hostile to small trains ahead of us. They were civil to us. On the north side of river above Falls is in every 1 mile a gushing springs. One falls from top of Bluff, 300 ft on straigh[t] wall & one mile above, on south side, and within a few rods of the river, is a Boiling spring—vary hot it is. To right of road in bend of river one mile off nearest point, cross creek, 50 ft wide, 4 miles above Falls. It is also the mouth of this stream.

August 6th. Tuesday. From the Salmon Falls you rise steep Bluffs of 2 miles, & heavy sand. Then to watering place, good level road; deep dust and sand; no grass. We travel'd this in the night and got to water at daylight this morning. From here to 3 Islands, 13½ miles. The first fine, vary hilley & crooked; then four level, and the last four & half hilley. Two steep hills to desend & one to assend; the first is to get to dry revene whare road forks. The right goes to camp on river, the left is the main road & two miles the nearest and will make camp & water at 3 Isl'ds nearly as soon. The last hill to desend is to get on river bottom at 3 Isl'ds. Heavy sand road the last 13½ miles. Thare is, on the last 6 miles some grass, but vary poor; it is the sedge grass. The 3 Islands have a delightful grass on them, and a good crossing in the river to get to them. At ordinary water you can ford to them at any place opposite. Good grass on main shore, next road. Here is whare the old road crosses river. The bottom is narrow on river. South side inclosed by high sand bluffs. We arrived here at noon today and drove stock on Island and lay balance of day. The road down on opposite side of river is said to be nearest, but the delay in making two crossings is not sufficient to justify unless a vary great Emigration. Then it would devide the feed which is about equal on either road. The country has not changed in character. In sight snow on Mts.

August 7th. Wednesday. Lay at 3 Islands.

August 8th. Thursday. Lay at 3 Islands.

August 9th. Friday. Left camp on route. 1 & 2 miles below 3 Islands, good camp and some grass. Between this and Dry Branch, which is from 3 Islands 7 miles, good camp at it. Good camp on road by side of river 2½ miles below. The road runs on river bank to Dry Branch & for 6 miles below; road sandy and on side hill below Dry Branch. 2 miles vary rocky on Mt side at edge of river; road vary narrow; drive with care. We camp for noon 2½ miles below Dry Branch and from thare to Lake or slough of river, vary heavy sand road. From Dry Branch to Lake or slough of river, 12 miles. Good place to camp. The Bluffs on the south side of Snake River runs out for six miles & receeds back. Thare is no Bluff on river at slough. Thare is a large & fine Isl'd formed by this slough. At head of slough, 2 & 3 miles off are vary high drifts of sand; vary singular, and 75 or 80 ft high. This cuntry still produces nothing but sage other than what grass mentioned; no timber at all. The Bluffs on the north side of river—this side south today—have had a gradual steep or incline; the decomposed parts forming a gradual slope, but vary steep. We campt on Lake or Slough of River. Travel from 3 Islands to camp, 20 miles. To whare road strikes Slough from 3 Islands, 19 miles.

August 10th. Saturday. From head of Slough or Lake of Snake River to crossing of River 50 ft wide, 2 ft deep, 7¾ miles. You travel down slough 3 miles, then leave it. Good camp whare you leave. You then gradually assend and desend a hill to the crossing of this River, distance given. Good camp on it any place near road. The bluffs are vary full of small round gravel—composed of such—before you get to this river. Road good; no grass at all on it from whare it leaves Slough to crossing. Crossing good, as stream is clear gravel bottom & lowe banks. Plenty willow, no other wood. You travel down this after crossing, 1 mile, then you have a gradual hill to assend to whare road strik[s] Snake River. ½ mile below whare the river you last crossed empties into Snake River is good camp, and up the river is vary good. The land does not produce a spear of grass. None as far as you can see off from road on the highland. Not much sage here. Distance from Last crossing River to whare road strikes Snake R., 6¼ miles. Good place to camp. We campt here. The road here keeps down River and a short distance from it, and at bends nears river. Road level and good. No grass at all—perfectly barren except a diminitive shrub in bunches. 6¼ miles down from last camp is anither good camp to right, whare road nears the river; this is on main shore, and thare is good camp on Island opposite.

The crossing to Island good. No camping place between them, nor further on, until you strike Mt. Stream. Good camp 1¾ miles from camp on River Bank & Island.

August 11th. Sunday. We passed yesterday on River, a train of Emigrants from Mo., that had 3 horses stolen from them the night before by the Indians. The wether vary warm. Thare has bin but few places on south side of Snake River in yesterday & to day that had any steep bluffs. They have receeded gradually back to level plane which runs to foot of Mt many miles back on the north side. They are not as abrupt and have bin gradually falling. At this Mt. stream we campt this night. Plenty wild rye & small cane grass; no other. Plenty willow for wood. At the crossing of this stream it is 6 ft wide, 6 in. deep. To the right is a high cliff of vary black rock forming a mound appearance as it stands by itself from any other range, and starts up from a level flat of high table land which is of a burnt ash surface and produces nothing but a few mean shrubs. To right of road & opposite crossing is a mass of black cliffs, some forming monuments to the highth of 50 ft. The last 11¾ miles and the next 8 to Caddle Creek, road good. Dust deep but not heavy. The last 3 miles to Caddle Creek you pass through a deep bason formed by high cliffs, vary broken by many revenes. The bluffs are based on a soft clay rock and after approaching towards top, sets in a black and red strata of volcanic rock—looks as if it had bin deposited during time when the Earth had bin covered in water. Caddle Creek, 6 ft wide, 6 in. deep, is not a vary good camp. It is a vary narrow revene making through a deep canyon. You do not see Snake river in next 26 miles from whare you leave to make Mt. stream. The country is of more appearance of fire than the last few days travel of 50 miles.

August 12th. Monday. We traveled from Mt. stream to Caddle Creek 8 miles. Poor camp at this time. No water between creeks. 14 miles from here before road strikes Snake River. Vary steep hill to assend from Caddle creek. After, road level, but deep dust. It strikes Snake River at mouth of Dry Branch after coming down it for 3 miles. No bluffs on south side of River whare road strike. Thare is a bluff to right of road below whare it strikes river, ½ mile, with a vary pirty tower or chimney by the side of it. Looks like a monument of Black Val'c rock. Vary warm to day. See some snow in drifts on Mt. west 10 miles off. No grass to feed a sheep on this days travel, except at places mentioned.

August 13th. Tuesday. From whare road strikes Snake River as above, it keeps down the river. Distance to next small creek, 6¼ miles. Plenty water above & below crossing. At the crossing, dry at this date. This is a first rate camp for 1 mile above and below crossing to river whare it empties; & on river below here we drove and remained for this day. The road is level, but deep dust and some sandy. No grass except some vary small strips on margin of the river between camps. But gradual hills on sides of river in place of former abrupt bluffs.

August 14th. Wednesday. From this Creek to Warm Springs, 3 miles. These Springs are to the left of the road, 150 yds, and vary flush. The water too hot to bear your hand in it. The branches from them run flush and cross the road opposite them. They are situated on a level bench or table, in a vary deep dust or Ashy ground, ½ mile from base of ridge. Road from creek level; heavy dust. From Springs to whare road has good camp on river, 11 miles. This is whare road leave river and take up gradual assend to left. The first 6 miles from Springs road level; then hill to assend & desend on bluff of river. This is a white clay bluff, and you will find many small hills between this and camp, which is situated as discribed. Whare road leaves river, and on the opposite side from this camp, on bottom some ¾ miles from river is a round black mound of rock standing by itself some distance from bluff. The road is also deep dust & sand. No grass on bench. Some small strips on the margin of the river. There could be some good camps for small parties within the last distance. The road will strike Snake River again in about six miles from whare it leaves. To crossing of Sturgeon Creek, 11 miles. Good camp at S. Creek, & for 5 miles before you get to it. Road level and generally good. A good quantity of bunch grass on road in last 8 miles growing on 2nd bottom on bench. We campt this night in the middle of this 11 mile strech on Snak[e] & Done well. Plenty Indians fishing on river here.

August 15th. Thursday. We traveled from camp. From Sturgeon Creek the road crosses bend of Snake. Level road, deep dust. To whare it strikes river again at bend, 3½ miles. Good camp. It then crosses bend again by turning to left. Good camping two and three miles from here on the road. Wild again near the river. Good bunch grass on the bench. Thare is no abrupt river bluffs on this part of road. From whare road nears the river, 3½ miles. From crossing of Sturgeon Creek—which is dry at this date, water only in holes—to crossing of the Owyhee River, which is 150 ft wide, 2 ft. deep, 12 miles. Good crossing and fine camp at any place on it to Fort Boise, which is 4 miles. You travel the first 9 miles of the last 12 on and near Snake River. The 3 miles before you reach the Owyhee is crossing ridge. Road all good, but heavy dust and some sand; and you travel down the Owyhee River to Fort Bosee on a splendid grass bottom the whole distance of 4 miles. The country is vary level around this place. Low banks of Snake River and some lowe bottom that produces good grass. The 2nd bench produces but vary little. We campt East of the fort on Snake this night [of the] 15th, about 9 miles.

August 16th. Friday. We come to Fort Bosee in morning & campt on bank of Owyhee whare road leaves it. Fort Bosee is another of these mud forts built by the Hudson Bay Co. It is 4 miles from the crossing of the Owyhee River to the Fort, and 15½ miles from the fort to Malheur River, which is the first water. The road by the Fort is 4 miles out of the way. It is only 15½ miles from the crossing of the Owyhee River by direct road leaving the fort to right. This fort is situated on the north bank of the River Snake. The road here leaves Snake River and takes west over a vary gradual roling cuntry. The road is good these 15½ miles, level and clear of much dust and sand. Good to camp at Malheur River any place, and plenty grass on the whole distance. We traveled this in the night of this day. The evening was vary fine and cool. This Malheur River is 80 ft wide, 18 in. deep gravel; pirty stream of clear water, running north-east. Plenty willow on its banks; no other wood. Bottom ¾ to 1 mile wide and has a vary heavy growth of wild Rye upon it. Whare we cross it tonight, the rocks have the apearance of being driven asunder from their original beds by some great comotion, with much the cast of fire on them. I caught up an Indian horse on graze here for a stray & took him in our camp. Some of them ware thare and near him. I returned him to them. We smoked together and departed in peace. This was on the morning of the 17th Aug. Hot spring at ford of this River.

August 17th. Saturday. From Malheaure River to Sulpher Springs 12¼ [miles]. Water healthy and good to use. Thare is not sufficient for large train to camp at. No grass only bunch grass on hill sides. Plenty wild sage for wood. Thare is 3 places these Springs brake out and sink in the distance of 100 yards leaving no water below them. The road from last river to these

Springs is first rate, following up a level bottom and branch all the way. Plenty of grass on this bottom, which is ¾ to 1 mile wide. There was no water in it at this date after you got 6 miles up it. The first 6 miles had some in pon[d]s or holes in it , but no running water. To the right of road 3 miles below the crossing of this river is a sugar loaf Mound or Mt of rock of vary great height seperated from the hills by the valley of this river. The hills on each side of this branch and valley are gradually roaling and covered with wild sage and bunch grass. Hard clay surface and no rock of any note on them. We campt this night after leaving last river at noon.

August 18th. Sunday. From Sulphur Spring to Birch Creek, 4 ft. wide, 6 in. deep, 10 miles. Good to camp at; bottom narrow. The road runs down it after crossing & leaves it near whare it emties into Snake River. From crossing of Birch Creek to whare the road strikes Snake River, 3½ miles. Good to camp at. Here you will leave Snake River imediately for the last time, as you will see it no more. It here wind[s] it[s] way through a ridge of high Mts., roling but not abrupt precipice, their surface covered with a red volcanic dust. The road from the Sulphur Springs to this place is hilly but not vary steep. The road is hard and good to travel. Plenty of bunch grass all the way growing on the rolling lands that you pass over. No fuel but sage and a few willow on creek. We campt at Birch Creek this day at noon, ½ mile below whare we crossed it, by side of a cliff of rock on the road; whare we remained until the morning of the 19th. We left the Horse Shoe Co. on Snake River below Sturgeon Creek & have not seen or heard of them since. We are camping alone. Driving but ½ the day to improve our stock.

August 19th. Monday. From the last of Snake River to Burnt River, 35 ft. wide, 1 ft. deep, 4½ miles. The road from Snake River to this is good. A long gradual hill to assend and desend to overcome the devide. Not vary steep. This brings you on to the bottom of Burnt River, which is a fine bottom of grass. The road follows up this river. You will have two steep points to cross in the first 3½ miles to save bends by river. Road good except round loose rock, which in places are plenty. Here you will cross a spring branch of cool water. The hills on each side, & roaling. Valley vary narrow. Thare is plenty of bunch grass on hills and good camp on bottom. Here we campt for this day & night after traveling from Birch Creek here.

August 20th. Tuesday. We travel up this river about 11 miles further. The road hilly and vary crooked. One vary steep hill half way. A man was found shot & is buried on this hill. We camped between 4th & 5th crossing at noon and remained until next morning. You cross this river 4 more times in the next 3 miles, which is at the crossing. You then take up a branch, 4 ft. wide, 6 in. deep, and in 2½ miles you will cross it 9 times, then raise a vary steep hill, ¾ mile up.

August 21st. Wednesday. We traveled on up to day about 17 miles and campt for the day. One steep Mt ½ way, and the last half of this days travel road vary good.

August 22nd. Thursday. Left camp 3 miles from last crossing of Burnt River. Traveled up to it and crossed Ridge to Powder River slough. See plenty snow from road to day. From [where] you first strike Powder River to last crossing at foot of vary steep hill, 34½ miles. You strike a spring branch 3 miles further that is of it. From hill to Powder River slough, 17 miles. You travel up this Burnt River 34½ miles on a road that is vary hilley and vary crooked. You are thrown often from the river and cross steep points of the Mt. to pass the Kanyons. You will fine plenty water up the hollows you take to cross these points. Thare is in all fine springs and fine grass. Good to camp at any short distance. The Mts. are vary steep. In many places you will find a quantity of Blue lime Stone rock, which is the principal rock that projects out of these Mts on this river. From the 6th to the 9th crossing you will pass a grove of Cotton Wood timber and some Birch. Thare is another grove to left of road on the river about 8 miles before you leave it. Thare is many branches near the head, and it is of one that the road [guide?] speaks of crossing, which is about 4 ft wide, 6 in. deep, at the foot of hill whare a lone ceder stands near road to left, half way up the hill & in view of crossing, 400 yards distant. Plenty camps any place & plenty fish.

[August 23rd. Friday.] From crossing last time Burnt River to Powder River, which is as has bin stated, 17 miles, you first assend steep hill ½ mile—which has the lone ceeder on it—and you then cross some roling ground, and at 3 miles you will strike spring branch that runs into powder river. This you follow to its head, about 1 mile, and in another mile you will rise the summit of a ridge and pass over some roling ground in the next

3 miles which will let you in a level bason. This you will travel to 3 miles of Slough of Powder River. Here you strike a level bottom & travel it until you cross Powder River, which is from Slough, 9¼ miles. In 3½ miles further cross branch of Powder River. The main river is 50 ft wide, 1 ft deep. The branch is 40 ft wide, 1 ft. deep.2 miles to another branch, dry at ford on this day, 23rd Aug. Plenty water above ford. ½ mile further fine spring. Here we campt this night. The road is vary good, level and plenty wood on creeks, and water. No water from Slough to river in 9¼ miles. See some fine Salmon in river. This river is in a circle and surrounded by some hills and Mts on all sides. These hills are not like Burnt River Mts. They do not produce but little grass. The bottom is large, and near the river and creeks produce abundance of vary fine grass. The Mts. west are covered with pine, vary fine; and some snow at this date upon them.

August 24th. Saturday. From Spring to Grand Round, 14½ miles. Good camp at grand round, and plenty water all the way on the road in a few miles, and plenty grass to camp at them. Some fine springs on the road. Road vary good until you get within 4 miles of grand round, then you have many loose rock and a vary steep hill to desend to valley, and vary rocky loose stone. Here we had a fine grove of pine to left of road 4½ miles before we arrived at grand Round and vary fine springs here. We found 3 of Uncle Sams waggons in grove. On the road side to right opposite is the grave of Amendy E.M. Right. Died 10th Sept., 1847. We campt at noon for balance of day on branch 4 ft wide, 4 in. deep, at foot of hill whare we first strike the valley of the grand Round. Thare is some quantity of projecting rock from the Mts on side of the road in this days travel, which are vary black and hard, and have much the cast of had bin burnt. The hills are vary gravely of this burnt rock and produce vary little grass. The timber is all pine, and growes in the revenes and high up on the sides of the Mts. and is vary tall and fine. It is of the white, and some yellow.

August 25th. Sunday. From whare you strike the valley of the Grand Round to Branch 2 ft wide, 3 in. deep is 7¼ miles. Here you leave the valley and assend a vary steep Mt, 1 mile long. The road is vary level and good to this place, and you can camp at spring near road on Mt side every ½ mile. Grass fine. This is a vary grand and fertile valley encircled by high Mts., round in shape and from 8 to 10 miles in diameter. The Mts., after they elevate from ½ mile to 1 mile from the level of the valley, are heavy clad with first rate pine, superior to any I see in the U.S. Through this valley passes Grand Round river, a stream 60 ft wide, 1 ft deep. Civilization at some day will reach this spot and cultivate it. Thare is many Indians about it, but harmless. From this valley to crossing Grand Round river by the road, 7½ miles. Vary steep Mt., as stated, to assend from valley and vary steep one also to desend to crossing of river. Road otherwise roaling. Many places small loose rock, but can be termed good. This is not good to camp at. Valley vary narrow and no grass on hills, nor water from valley here. Thare is thick pines at crossing, and much pine and vary fine on the road to crossing from the valley here. We traveled this day to this place, and remained until next day. A band of Kiuse Indians campt with us. All well.

August 26th. Monday. From crossing of Grand Round River to camp spring, 1st water, 20½ miles. These are the Blue Mts. Thare is a spring to left and a place off road at 13 miles from Round River, but hard for Emigrants to find. The first 13 miles is vary hilly road & 3 steep points of Mt to assend. The last 7½ to camp spring, road vary good; and a vary fine road for the next 14½ miles, whare you will strike a branch and fine springs to right of road. From Round River you will travel 30 miles through vary heavy thick timber of pine; vary fine and vary tall. Fine grass in places. Plenty Bear & some small game; plenty wolves. We campt at Grand Round River this night with a band of Kiuse Indians and their herd of 150 horses.

August 27th. Tuesday. We campt at Spring; Left road, 4½ miles from camp spring in Mt. These springs are on prairie and 4½ miles after you leave timber of Blue Mts. Road fine. Springs situated near foot of vary long hill. Here we found Encampt Mr. Wm. Craig,[11] a Mt man, born in Green Briar Co., Va., and who has bin in the Mts for 22 years. He is with the Ne Pusee Indians, & with him we traded our oxen & waggon for Horses. We traded 1 yoke oxen for horse. I traded my riding horse for his even. We traded goods for some other horses with the Kiuse Indians. With him was a Delewar Ind., James Simon. Mr. Craig is the man who saved Mrs. Spalding from the Whitman Massacre.

11 Craig was Agent to the Nez Perces.

August 28th, 29th, 30th. We lay campt with Mr. Craig and prepared our packs for Horses. On the 29th, 3 waggons belonging to the U.S., loaded with provisions for the relief of destitute Emigrants came and campt with us. Thare is plenty of upland dry grass here. 5 miles from this you near the Umatilla River opposite to Kiuse Indian village. You travel down from springs to crossing this river 14 miles. The grass grows fine, but has all bin eaten off, from the emense quantity of Horses grazed on it by the Kiuse Inds. About 8 miles from the spring you get into the Wala Wala Inds. From the first crossing of the Umatilla to whare it strikes the bottom of this river again is 20 miles. Good road and grass but no water. We traveled from springs to the river bottom here on this day.

August 31st, September 1st. We travel to Willow Creek on left hand road & campt on it 2 miles above crossing. Grass & good road all the way. From whare road strikes river bottom to fork of the road on north side river, six miles. It crosses imediately at forks. From thare to Willow Creek, 9 miles. Good grass. The right hand road keeps down Umatilla & crosses below.

September 2nd. Monday. This day we traveled to next creek, a willow creek. Water in holes. Distance 30 miles. Fine grass at it, and plenty of it. Thare is two well springs of Mineral water half way on the road, Good to use. They rise in top of small mound of their own formation and sink around in a short distance; but little to be depended upon for camp. Plenty of bunch grass in the first 15 miles of them, but little after you leave them until you reach the creek. At these springs is whare Geo. Gilam of Mo., was shot by accident in 1845 on his return to Oregon city from the Kiuse War; and at this place the Indians met the army in their advance on them. The Inds. had 2 men killed and retreated. This 30 miles of road is hilly & sandy, but can be termed a good road. On this nights camp on Willow Creek two of our horses to[ok] fright and run off. We were until 10 Ock next day finding them.

September 3rd. Tuesday. We traveled to branch of Jon Days river, 20 miles & campt on good grass. Thare is a small spring to right of road by some seeder to left, 2 miles before you get to this branch. The first 12 miles of this road is hilly & sandy, the balance vary level down lake that is dry in valley. The last 10 miles the cuntry has no grass and plenty precipices of black volcanic rock on sides of valley. The soil is burnt up.

September 4th. Wednesday. We traveled 6 miles down this branch & cross it 4 times. Road rocky in places but at its junction with John Days river. We cross river, good camp any place here in 7 miles from where you strike the branch. From crossing of Jno. Days River to whare road strikes the Columbia is 25 miles without water. Thare is a vary rocky hill and sandy to assend ¾ mile from Days river. The next 11 miles to junction of the river road is vary good. The balance to Columbia river is hilly & broken. You have a vary steep hill to desend to Columbia. From whare you strike the Columbia to De Shoot or Fall River is 3 miles down river bottom in heavy sand. This river you will ferry in canoes. It is kept by Ind's.Thare is fine bunch grass all the way from Days River. We campt this day whare road strikes Columbia.

September 5th. Thursday. We traveled to the Dalls. From Fall River to branch 10 ft wide 1 ft deep, 5 miles. Steep Mts to assend & desend to Branch. Plenty grass on branch & on road. 1½ miles to fine spring on road; good to camp & at this spring the road forks, the right by Dalls. From here to next creek 2½ miles. From Creek to Dalls 6 miles. You go down this creek 2 miles, then you are on Columbia, then down it to the Dalls. Good grass all the way. Road hilly until you get within 4 miles of Dalls.

September 6th. Friday. Traveled from Dalls to 3'd branch, 10 miles. There is fine grass here. The first branch is 5 miles, next 2, next 3. The road vary hilly then steep. This cuntry affords an abundance of bunch grass but most certainly if put to cultivation would be unproductive, as the soil is light dust and sand, & in the dry season has no moisture; which is the general character of all the land from the Dalls until you strike the timber at the foot of the Caskade Mountains. The Dalls is situated at the head of Caskade Mts on the Columbia River. It has no improvements but one vary indifferent house for the commissary. There is 3 Co's of soldiers here tented in camp. They are engaged in building of a saw mill at this time to facilitate the anticipated improvement by the government. The river cliffs are black rock and vary rugged and steep perpendicular from the waters edge. Many of the Emigration have delay'd here. Many gone to work for the gov'mt. The most of all the Emigration are out of provisions and have to be furnished by the troops. The boats that run the river to this place are battaus rowed by 6 men, which is the only craft that can with any facility navigate the river here. The Columbia River here is a poor thing. Thare is plenty of Salmon caught out of it here and above & on all its branches by the Ind's, which is their principal living. They sell them at $1 apiece; or a Shirt for a Salmon.

September 7th. Saturday. We traveled only 5 miles to another creek 10 ft wide, 1 ft deep which brought us to the junction of the road again, which is by the cross cut from whare we left it at spring , 12 miles. This creek has a fine little valley of excellent grass. Thare is a fine bunch grass all the way from here to the next creek, which is 15 miles. [It] is a fine creek 30 ft wide, 1 ft deep. This is a prong of De Shoot River. We cross it at the old Indian village, at this time avacuated. The road is vary good, roaling, but none steep except a long hill to desend; this is steep. To get down to this creek you will pass through a point of timber about ¾ mile. About 9 miles from this creek the principal growth is pine; there is some scrubby white oak. Between this and the Dalls, on side of creek, is a few trees of this oak, which is the first I see on the road from Fort Larame. From this creek vary steep hill to assend 12 miles, 1 to desend to creek 6 ft wide, 1 ft deep. You will assend gradual hill and travel vary good road a cross another creek 4 ft wide, 6 in. deep in 6 miles. Here you strike the Pine timber & a few white oak — vary scrubby. Travel through this 4 miles on good road, some loose rock, to creek 10 ft wide, 1 ft deep, which is at foot of Mt. Here we campt on this Evening.

September 8th. Sunday. 10 miles S.E., Mt. Hood, which is covered with snow.

September 9th. Monday. We traveled to branch No. 2, west of Summit two miles, on good grass left of road. Distance of this days travel 28 miles made up as follows:

> From foot of Mt to Clear Creek, 10 ft wide, 18 in
> deep; steep hill to desend 6
> Small Creek 10 ft wide, 1 ft deep; steep hill to
> desend & assend 1
> Small Creek, 6 ft wide, 6 in. deep 2
> Muddy Creek, 30 ft wide, 18 in. deep; vary bad
> hill des'd 3

To camp between 5th & 6th crossing 5
To 7th crossing 1
Here you leave and take up to left of Creek of
clear fine water, and cross it between here
and the 2nd old House 7 times, which
is 6
From Old House to Summit 2
½ mile of this vary steep to assend and road
rough through heavy timber for the last
8 miles.
From Summit to Creek 10 ft wide, 1 ft
deep 1½
All this distance vary steep to des'd heavy
timber.
To Creek No. 2, 10 ft wide, 1 ft deep . . . . ½

September 10th. Tuesday.
To Prairie cross ridge & Swamp 2
To Prairie cross rid[g]e to Creek 3
To top of Mt. Steep ass'd & des'd 2
To Top Laurel Hill. Steep 2
To Foot. Vary steep & bad to des'd 2
To Branch of Sandy, 30 ft wide, 2 ft deep 2
To 4th Crossing. Road vary rocky & sandy 4
To 5th Crossing. Road vary rocky & sandy 5

We campt this evening three miles above the 5th crossing of this creek.
Here the woods has bin burnt and much timber bin destroyed. The timber
is principaly fur & pine, and vary tall, 200 & 250 ft. The _____[?] of Laurel
Hill I see 70 _____[?] by the side of a fallen tree; the top was lost. This place
west side, vary tall timber.

September 11th. Wednesday. We traveled from 3 miles below the 5th
crossing of Sandy to the 6th crossing as follows:
From 5th crossing to whare road leaves
Sandy 4
To foot of hill through rich bottom 1
Cross hill to 6th crossing 8

The hill is good to assend; short and not steep. You travel on good level ridge and vary rich land to crossing. Steep hill to des'd, but good. This land has a vary luxurant growth of Ferrens and pine & Furr timber in abundance. This will eventually be settled. The soil is vary red. Cuntry vary rolling.

September 12th. Thursday. To Foster's, the first House in Willamette valley, 10 miles from Sandy. This we made by noon to day & traveled 4 [miles]. Campt at Cook's Farm 8 miles further. We are now through in the valley.

September 13th. Friday. Remained in camp. Went to Oregon City during day & back to camp.

September 14th. Saturday. Struck camp & moved up valley to John Nelson on Bute Creek, a branch of the Nolealey, 30 miles above Oregon City. Here I stay until the 23rd to graze horses. On the 23rd, I went to Cuttings Saw Mill, & stay with John H. Frush, whare he is engaged at $5 per day & borded, to attend mill.

September 24th. I stay all night at Milwakie. My Bill $2.50

September 25th. I came to Portland, whare I got in with Col. W.M. King, my old Friend.

J. Knotts boats ferryed persons from Each Shore across the Willamotte River at Portland on the 27th 28th days of Decr and on the 29th. I was present at his leaving the shore at the old Ferry landing with his boat, he steering with ola hand (his boy) with him with the boat loaded with seven head cattle and two other men crossing them to Portland. Wm Stephens was with me and warned him of what was doing.

Wm H Frush

Decr 31 (1850). J Knotts ferried W H [Frush] in from Portland with his horse and ferry, 3 men back in same boat from opposite side to Portland.

1851 Jany 1st. Knotts boat ferryed one mare and man and horse from opposite Portland to Portland. 2nd man & horse from P twice skift & 2 men from P[ortland].

Jany 4. J. Knotts Binyaro Knote & _______ came over with guns & pistols and assaulted and attepted to shoot Stephens & took a man from his shore.

Jany 11th. James Mills toke down Stephens fence and made threats to do so on the 12th when I prevented him in the act. Wm H. Frush

Jany 22, 23, 24 & 25th. I was not at home to see if Knotts ferried.

March 4th (1851). Joseph Knotts with armed force of 8 or nine men landed at the Ferry Landing which I run Boats from and attended to and informed me of their intention to Land at my Landing at my defiance unless I would pull down the fences of the enclosure to Mr. Stephens Farm. I objected to them landing and refused to open the fence. He then returned to Portland with part of his mob and left a part on my side which was armed with guns & he immediately returned with 7 or eight more and ordered me on his approach to the landing to move my boat off the landing, if not he would and commanding to remove them thereafter off the landing so soon as I had made the landing. I objected to doing either and to his landing. He nevertheless landed and approached me with threats of abuse. My brother interfered for my safety. He aimed a revolver on him — I seized his arm from shooting he then with his mob went into my house and there in most ruffin like shook his fist in my face and meny threats of abuse to me with challenge to fight me with guns pistols knives

45

or clubs or fist and kucles. Replied I was no ruffin. He remained several hours with his mob and never ceased in language to abuse me in the most ruffin like manner, and after leaving the shore with his men and boat raising yell and fired a salute of 20 or 30 rounds.

March 7. Knotts manned his boat with four men and forced my boat from coming to my landing.

March 14. Col Backenstach stated to me that the Ferry man on Cosfinsg & Cacferry showed him his pistols and agreed to land him at our landing with his life. Col B said he saw the arms —

Decr 14th (1852). Tuesday night of December the 14th the snow at Portland, Oregon Territory. 15th and 16th it fell to the depth of 10 or 11 inches it then snow every day or night until the 23rd. On this day it snowed all day and with the fall of snow since the 14th which has remained on the ground since it is about 16 inches deep on this morning. The Willamotte River at Portland is entirely covered with mush ice. This is a desperate time on stock and much must perish. On the 21st *Dr. Shang* and 6 other lay on the Columbia River at Cape Horn Mt the Piper froze to death the ballance all froze more or less. On the 26th of December the snow fell all day on the previous snow and at night of this day it is about two feet deep. The 27th it moderated and rained all day and removed most of the ice in the Willamotte River at Portland O. T., which has been so much that it has been impossible with any thing but skifts to ferry and vary hard to cros with them the Chehalis Mt is represented to have 4 ft snow on it. Much stock of every kind are dying for want of feed as this is unusual and persons ware not prepared. The Emegration of this year must meet with a vary serious loss —

A TRIP FROM
THE DALLES, OREGON
TO FORT OWEN, MONTANA

BY

CHARLES FRUSH

YE GALLEON PRESS
FAIRFIELD, WASHINGTON 99012

Charles W. Frush seems to have had wandering feet in the pioneer west. Following the example of his uncle, W. H. Frush, who came across the plains to Oregon in 1850, young Charles followed in 1853. While the uncle came by wagon train Charles took the easier route of traveling by sea to Panama, crossing the isthmus on board a somewhat reluctant mule, then by ship to San Francisco and apparently on to Portland, Oregon.

Highlights of Charles Frush's Experiences
in the Pacific Northwest

1853	Came West.
1858	Emplyee of John Owen — trader in charge of commisary.
1860	At Lapwai acting as Sub Agent for Nez Perces.
winter 1862-63	At Flathead Agency on tributary of Jocko River.
1863	With G. J. Sherwood who ran an express between Walla Walla and Fort Benton and Bannack.
1880	Contractor, lived Portland, Oregon.
1881	Agent, Walla Walla & Colfax Stage Coach Co.
1883	Clerk, Land Dept., NPRR, lived Portland.
1884	Deputy Marshal, U. S. Court, lived Portland.
1886	Deputy Marshal, U. S. Court, lived Portland.
1887-88	Deputy, U. S. Marshal, Portland.

A TRIP FROM THE DALLES OF THE COLUMBIA, OREGON, TO FORT OWEN, BITTER ROOT VALLEY, MONTANA, IN THE SPRING OF 1858.

BY CHARLES W. FRUSH

In the month of May, 1858, the little town of the Dalles was all that a frontiersman would desire — a regular "hurrah camp." Pack trains, miners' and quartermasters' wagon trains were preparing to start, some on very long journeys into the heart of a hostile, savage country. All was mirth and merriment, no one appearing to care for or fear the dangers that lay across the trail. Among the many parties packing bucking "cayuses" and braying mules that beautiful spring day were two that had long, wearisome marches ahead of them. One was the Hudson's Bay "brigade" of seventy-five packs in charge of a Mr. Oglesby, with George Montour, a half-blood, as interpreter, and ten Colville Indians as packers and herders, on its way to the Hudson's Bay Company's Fort Colville on the banks of the mighty Columbia River, near Kettle Falls. The other was a government outfit composed of sixty-five head of animals, about twenty-five with packs and the balance loose, in charge of Major John Owen, of Fort Owen, who had been appointed United States Indian agent for the Flathead, Upper and Lower Pend d'Oreille, and Kootenai tribes or bands of Indians, with your humble servant as a kind of brevet Second Lieutenant in command of the mess box, which, of course, contained the "wherewith," the decoction made to get up a little "Dutch courage" with in tight places, and I assure you that box was watched with an "Argus eye." In addition there was a colored boy for cook and four Flathead Indian packers. When the words "All ready!" were given we mounted, and for awhile there was some lively bucking and stampeding, but after the first day's drive the ponies were all very docile.

Our trail was what early pioneers knew as the "Buffalo trail," and was used by the Indians from this side who made yearly trips to the east of the Rocky Mountains. It crosses the Des Chutes River near its confluence with the Columbia, thence over the rolling prairie, crossing John Day River, and on to the banks of the Columbia again, which it traverses to the mouth of Snake River where the Northern Pacific Railroad has a fine bridge, but at that time ferryboats and bridges were scarce articles, and here the trouble began. There was no drift or timber anywhere in sight to make a raft, and the Indians, what few were left in their camp, were sulky and did not seem disposed at first to ferry us over in their canoes, but after a little "wah-wah," or talk, they consented and we drove the animals, after unpacking, into the swift waters of the Snake which was about half a mile wide, very rapid and with the spring rise just commencing, but all safely landed on the other side; then with the aid of eight or ten canoes we soon had over all the stores and "riggin" and of course felt much elated over our good luck and sent our old Walla Wallas back with their canoes well pleased and with a "close-tum-tum" (good heart towards us for the liberal amount of tobacco we gave them for their services).

May 30, 1858. We traveled along the Columbia River, over a sage brush flat, for some twenty miles and camped on its banks near the White Bluffs. This evening we heard startling news. A Nez Perce chief, named Jesse, came to our camp, and through George Montour, the Hudson's Bay Company's interpreter, we learned of the great battle Colonel Steptoe had had with the Indians out on the prairie near a butte (now known as Steptoe's Butte) in Whitman County, Washington Territory.[1] This county was then looked upon as a wild waste, but to-day (1885) is one of the finest agricultural counties in Washington. This news gave us the "blues," especially the fact that the soldiers were defeated, Captain Taylor and Lieutenant Gaston killed and also a number of privates. The whole command retreated to Walla Walla leaving the Indians masters of the country, and the very country we had to go through.

At this camp I experienced my first game of bluff played with Indians. About dark some seven or eight canoes loaded with Yakima warriors landed near our camp. They were painted and rigged up in first-class war style and just spoiling for a fight. Our few Indian packers and the interpreter took the situation in and suggested that we bluff them. So we built a large camp fire out of sage brush and grease wood, and all of us, the Major included, formed a circle and with one hand holding a raw-hide, with a stick in the other, batted that raw-hide and yelled and danced until we were nearly exhausted. This act, the interpreter said, was intended to show these Yakimas that we were not afraid of them and were ready to give them "the best we had in the shop," and to my utter surprise when I turned out in the morning not a canoe was to be seen. It was a complete bluff. They had taken the hint and gone away during the night. I must confess I felt pleased, and so would any one, from the fact that there is less danger in thumping the raw-hide, as a bluff, than trying to dodge their bullets.

The animals were driven into camp and packed and we started, and nothing transpired during the two days following until we reached the Spokane River, near its mouth, very near to where Camp Spokane — a six company post — is now located. On arriving here we learned there had been a fight between a large party of miners, who started from The Dalles for the Frazer River country via the Okanagan canon, and the Okanagans, their chief, Quilt-ta-mina, being killed.

This was a serious affair to us, and, if it had not been for the influence held by Montour, the half-blood with these people, your writer would not now be penning these lines. We were allowed, however, to move camp unmolested, but a fearful yell of defiance met our ears from forty or fifty painted hostile savages, who, I presume, thinking we might not appreciate their clemency, rode along on either side of our party for some distance, and kept up their war-whoop to remind us that we were getting off cheap. We were not troubled any more that day, and made about twenty miles and camped. The next day was Sunday, and with good luck we hoped to reach the Hudson's Bay Company's Fort Colville, which we were heading for, so as to have the company of the company's brigade and their interpreter, George Montour, a valuable and trustworthy man. This route, to be sure, was hundreds of miles out of our way, but under the circumstances we deemed it the best, thinking we would miss the Indians, who would be out on the prairie near where the battle had been fought. But we did not rightly guess, for we jumped out of the frying-pan into the fire.

The war party, after the fight and when they found out next morning that the soldiers had retreated during the night towards Walla Walla, gathered up their trophies and came to the Hudson's Bay Company's post at Colville to have their grand war-dance and count their *coups*, and we arrived at the fort on that Sunday, which I am sure I will not forget. It was an Indian circus. They were having the finest "pic-nic" they had had for a long time. I have seen many an Indian war-dance since, and have had a great deal of experience with the Indians, but I have never seen anything that equalled this affair. A great many of them were entirely nude, some painted half red and half black, and some daubed all over with white mud, a kind of pipe clay, and then spotted with red. All were armed with Hudson Bay guns, rifles, or with bows and arrows, and were drumming and singing, with an old hag in the center of a circle they had formed, who would recite the daring feat some brave had performed and, shaking in the faces of the warriors the swords and pistols and other trophies they had taken from the officers and men killed in the fight, tantalize them by telling them to go and do better.

Here we met Mr. Thomas Harris and wife, and Henry M. Chase, wife, and two children, who had accompanied Major Owen from Fort Owen on their way from Walla Walla and the Dalles, but fearing Indian troubles thought it best to stop at Fort Colville, until the Major returned. And here it is proper to say a word or two relative to the hospitality and bravery of the Chief Trader Angus McDonald, a Highland Scotchman, who was in charge of the post. During the time we were his guests he gave Major Owen free use of any of the buildings for our little party to camp in, which of course we gladly accepted, for one feels a little more safe in a log shanty, no matter how dilapidated, than in a tent pitched in the midst of five hundred or six hundred hostiles, who were in the mood to shoot an arrow into a "Boston" (white man) just for the sake of seeing him wiggle. Now the grave question arose, how were we to get out of the Colville valley without being set afoot, as we were satisfied they did not intend to massacre the party on account of existing circumstances; that is to say, several of the party had half-breed wives who, with their children, were distantly related, and with an Indian, relationship goes a long way back where with us it would have become extinct. The Major appointed a day for us to make a start and it was understood we should leave at daybreak in order that the "red devils" might be caught napping. The stock was driven into the Hudson's Bay Company's stockade corral in the morning. I was up while the stars were shining and quickly had our pack-animals packed, and every one was in the saddle when the train, about fifteen or twenty packs, and some forty loose animals — horses and mules — quietly moved out of the corral and headed up the Colville valley towards the Spokane country. When the Major tied his fine saddle mule — Kitty — to a post in front of the Chief Trader's house and went in to speak to Mr. McDonald, a big brave, an Okanagan, deliberately walked up, untied the mule, and unceremoniously walked off with the rope — and the mule also. Old Angus McDonald, looking out of his window, saw this bold proceeding, rushed out of the house and across the court-yard, snatched the rope from the Indian, and gave him a severe lecture in his own language relative to his conduct, unbecoming an Indian brave and more especially so in regard to the respect due him — Angus McDonald, the Chief Trader of the Hon. Hudson's Bay Company's Post — giving him to understand that no such business would be tolerated. You should have seen the Major smile when the old Glencoe chieftain led the mule, Kitty, back and handed her over to her owner, who valued the mule and outfit at $500.00.

After traveling about one mile from the fort, I put the animals, packs and all, into a dead run, but in a little while heard that ominous yell and, looking back, saw the red devils coming. When they caught up with the train, they dashed right through it, thinking to stampede the animals, who kept to the trail however. The Indians then commenced to throw the lariat and, after lassoing seven or eight head, took their prizes, silently dropped out and disappeared. I kept on that day to the farm house of Thomas Strenger, having made about thirty miles. Here we found that several families — settlers — had taken refuge under the hospitable roof of Mr. Strenger. He was a Scotchman by birth and an old resident of the valley. His wife was an Indian woman of the Spokane tribe, and her people exercised large influence with the hostiles who of course respected everything about the ranch of Mr. Strenger; hence those that put themselves under his protection were not harmed. We camped near his house for the night and were not molested by the redskins. The next morning found us in the saddle bright and early, with a long day's drive before us. Night brought us to the Little Spokane River where all was quiet and serene and we indulged in a good night's rest, but in the morning a war party of Spokanes and Kalispels came to our camp and had a long talk and smoke among themselves relative to the Major; whether or not they should keep him or kill him, but after a lengthy "pow-wow" they concluded to let us go, though they said (so the women of our party

55

interpreted to us) that Major Owen had big eyes and big hands, that he said and wrote bad things about them to the "Great Father" at Washington and it was better such things should be stopped. During the talk they took the Major's saddle animal and tied her near their camp, but afterwards an Indian brought the mule back and tied her at our camp, and we all drew another long breath and satisfied ourselves (by feeling) that the hair was still on our heads, though the Major would have lost a few silver threads only.

Well, thanks to some guardian angel or "big medicine," we got away from Little Spokane all right and the train started over the divide for the old Kalispel Mission on the Pend d'Oreille River, where we arrived after a tedious day's drive and camped on the west bank of this beautiful stream — Clark's Fork of the Columbia. On its east bank, some forty miles below Lake Pend d'Oreille, the Jesuit Fathers had a mission, known as the Kalispel Mission, which was abandoned years ago. At this place a few friendly Kalispels assisted the party very much and were well paid for the services rendered, for without the aid of their bark canoes, I scarcely know how we would have made the seventy-five or eighty miles to the Cabinet mountains or head of the lake, for it was now summer and the lake was bankfull. Major Owen, Tom Harris and Henry M. Chase unfortunately could not swim, necessitating the use of a canoe for each of them and their families, whilst I, in charge of the pack-train with a few Indians to help, drove along the lake shore and thought it lucky when we touched bottom, for at least two-thirds of the way the whole train was either wading in mud and water or swimming. We were three or four days in reaching the head of the lake, and as it was warm and pleasant it did not take long to dry what little wearing apparel we had on, and we were also happy to think we had this large expanse of water between us and those cut-throats, the Spokane and Coeur d'Alene Indians, who were mean enough to scalp a man for almost nothing, even a bald headed man like Major Owen. We were now about out of their country and all feeling a little spunky, though on rather weak diet as they had stolen our principal packs, mules, saddles and all, including our provisions, but there was that never failing substitute — berries; service berries, blue berries, whortle berries and choke cherries. The service berries, boiled with a little buffalo fat and flour, make a very good meal, sufficiently nutricious (sic) to put one in condition to endure a long day's ride, but a person becomes tired of such fare very soon.

Our trail now followed the Pend d'Oreille River — Clark's Fork of the Columbia — to Horse Plains, or where the Flathead and Missoula Rivers join, which point all old pioneers consider to be the head of the River Pend d'Oreille. Our slow traveling with tired animals and riders along the shady mountain trail brought us to what was considered the country of the Flatheads where we felt secure, for they were particular friends of the Major and the families of some of our party. At Horse Plains, the junction of the Flathead and Missoula Rivers, we tarried two days to allow our animals to rest and feed, for the grass was fine and I am sure they needed it as some of them had been tied up night after night and were looking very thin. Here we met Michael Ogden and a small party of Indians — Mission Pend d'Oreilles — who evinced great delight on finding our party all safe, as they had feared the hostiles might have taken us in, and who furnished us a part of their provisions which was very acceptable. That day's drive was more merry, everyone in good spirits, and even the poor tired animals realized the fact that they were on more hospitable ground where they could graze undisturbed. At last we crossed Cammas (sic) Prairie, and were safely over the Flathead River, a little above the mouth of the Jocko, and now took the trail to St. Ignatius Mission.

Arriving at the mission we were met by the good fathers, who kindly welcomed us back and soon had our camp supplied with plenty of good things. The genuine kindness, unsolicited, from these missionaries, I am sure the writer will ever gratefully remember. As near as I can recollect, Father Hoecken was the Superior in charge of the mision, and with him were Fathers Mennetrey and Gazzoli. After another day's rest we started on the "home drive" to Fort Owen in the Bitter Root valley, about seventy-five miles distant. Our trail took a southerly course to the beautiful valley of the Jocko, thence up said valley and through the Coriacan (also spelled Koriaken) Defile to the bottom lands in the Hell Gate Ronde where the grass was luxuriant and here we camped in peace. The next day's march took us across the Hell Gate River and as far as the Lo Lo Fork. Our last day's march brought us to the long looked for haven, Fort Owen; and after a lapse of twenty years I can see those old *adobe* walls and buildings as distinctly as if it were but yesterday. When the party reached the fort, Mr. Caleb E. Irvine, who had been left in charge, and a few *attaches* of the fort, ran out to welcome us, and general hand shaking and congratulations ensued.

(The names of some of the pioneers of this section and where they were located, I will give as near as I can remember.) There were camped in the immediate vicinity of Fort Owen the following: Fred Burr, Thomas Adams, "Reece" (Rezin) Anderson, Captain Richard Grant and family, David Petty and John Powell; those living at Fort Owen were Major John Owen, Thomas Harris and wife, Caleb E. Irvine and family, Henry M. Chase and family, John Silverthorne and the writer. Old hunters who had located farms and settled in the Bitter Root valley were Mr. Lumphrey, Al. Talman, a Frenchman called "Johnny Crappeaux," and an old Mexican named Emanuel, and there was one settler in the Hell Gate Ronde named Brooks. In the fall of '58 a couple of Frenchmen from Colville valley whose names were Louis Brown and "Crooked-hand" Shaw camped in the Jocko valley, and shortly afterwards moved over to what is now known as Frenchtown, in Missoula County.

I will now bring to a close this brief sketch of the dangers and hardships incident to the settlement of our frontier. To those who experienced them I am sure they were of such character as to leave a lasting impression in their memories.

A TRIP FROM FORT OWENS IN THE
BITTERROOT VALLEY TO FORT BENTON,
ON THE MISSOURI RIVER IN
THE WINTER OF 1858.

BY CHARLES W. FRUSH

A TRIP FROM FORT OWENS IN THE BITTERROOT VALLEY TO FORT BENTON, ON THE MISSOURI RIVER IN THE WINTER OF 1858.

BY CHARLES W. FRUSH

Along in the month of November 1858, the Major "John Owen" gave orders to bale up all the Furs some 200 # consisting of Beaver, Bear, Mink, Martin and Fisher, which were done up in 50# bales — and when done the animals were got up and the saddles selected. For them nothing but the old fashioned Pack Saddles was used with the "Cinch" and fastening strap so that each side pack was cinched on the same as one would fasten his riding saddle, which style for light packing is much more simple and quicker than with the Apparajo and diamond hitch — no sling or lash ropes to be used. So your writer was instructed to put up rations for five men for twelve days which amount was ample, so the Maj. said, but which we found out to our sorrow to be insufficient.

The party consisted of Maj. John Owen, C. W. Frush, "Francoise" the Interpreter, and two Flathead Indians, packers, and when everything was ready the Maj. gave the Command to march in genuine military style, and so we turned our backs on Fort Owen. One of those beautiful November days that Montana is blessed with, the air clear and crisp, our first day's drive was to Lo Lo's Fork. When we got 7 or 8 miles from Fort Owen we met Angus McDonald, Son, and his faithful Indian Coulto from Colville, on their way to the Buffalo Country to meet his family, his wife, 2 daughters and 2 sons who had gone on a Hunt with their relatives, Old Bonapart and Michel Ogden and Ambrose's the Pend d'Oreille chief's Party. So the Maj. and myself were much pleased to have the company of the old Highlander and his Son an Indian hunter but they would have to go to Victor's Camp, the Flathead Chief, who was camped near Fort Owen on the banks of the lovely Bitter Root River, to get fresh Horses, and the

Maj. went back with them saying they would overtake us next day at the Mouth of the Big Blackfoot River. So I camped with my party the first night at Lo Lo's Fork. The next day's drive brought us to the Big Blackfoot. At that time there was but one settler in the Hell Gate Ronde; that was a Mr. Brooks known to the pioneers by his Indian name 'Stillocshun" who had an Indian Woman for his Wife who lived about one mile from where the trails crossed the Hell Gate River going from Fort Owen to the Flathead Missions north of said River. After I had been in camp two days the Maj. sent an Indian Messenger to me with a note stating he and MacDonald and party would be camp next day. Well, that was 5 days that we had been drawing on our original 12 days rations, and on the evening of the 5th day they arrived. I remarked to the Maj., did you bring more rations. He replied, No, what do we want to bother our heads about rations for when we have got the finest shot and hunter in the Rocky Mountains, Angus McDonald. He will kill more game than we can pack — and in those days game was plenty and not wild. Now we start up the Big Blackfoot for "Cadotts" Pass on the Rocky Mountains; well, during the 3 jor 4 days we were making the distance to the sumit nothing transpired worthy of mention. The Glencoe Chief killed an old Honker Goose, fat and tough. We boiled him all night so that we could masticate him and that helped a little for the day, for Mac did not hunt much off the trail as he was very fond of taking an Ice Bath in the Blackfoot River every morning. The River was frozen over except in the Middle where there was an open channel of swift running water, and of course, as cold as charity.

After the Indians would have a large Camp fire built he, MacDonald, would disrobe, walk down the bank in the Snow, for there had fell a few inches, and sit down on the Ice, slide out to the open water and roll in like a Beaver puff and splash for a while and then back to the Fire, Wrap a Blanket about him and stand before it and steam himself. This, he said, would make a man hardy enough to stand the Cold of the Arctic but I did not indulge, and I think I could stand as much cold as Mr. Mac D. Well, now we are on the summit of the old Rockies, Cadotts Pass, the Head Waters of the Big Blackfoot River, the snow getting pretty deep up here, but only extending a little way down the Eastern slope where the Buffalo Grass is fine and the "Paradise" of the beautiful Antelope of which bands can be seen feeding in almost any direction. Away to our right as we strike a Bee line for Sun River stands the noted Land Mark known as Bird-tail

Rock, looming up in the clear atmosphere and to all appearance only a mile or two off, but in reality some 25 miles away. Last night we ate the last of our provisions, but with our Hunters and the the great number of Antelope in sight, the thoughts of hunger did not disturb us during the day as Mac Donald and his Indian Coulto started for the bands of Antelope with the understanding that they would come to our Camp, which would be on Sun River, and we were aiming to strike the River about 25 miles above where the old Fort Benton trails cross it, having heard that Col. Vaughn, the Agent for the Blackfoot tribes, was camped in Sun River Valley some distance up towards its head, hence our reason for taking this course. And, after a very hard days drive, we reached the River about dark. Both men and beasts tired out, all too glad to get out of a saddle, and, I am sure, the poor dumb brutes glad to be relieved of their burdens and given a chance to pick a little grass. But for ourselves, we had to be content to sit down and enjoy a smoke on an empty stomach for we had nothing to eat and no MacDonald or Indian Hunter. And, we had built a large Camp Fire to draw their attention if they were in sight, but they did not find us that night and, of course, we rolled up in our robes and went to sleep without our much promised "Antelope" steak and "Rib Roasts" for supper.

The next morning we saddled up and started down the Valley of Sun River and after a 3 or 4 hours drive we came to the old Cols. Camp, and in a short time Mr. MacD and his Indian arrived in camp, all O.K., but nary an "Antelope" and hungry tired. They discovered that an Antelope can beat a poor tired Horse and not half try. But the genial "Old Agamemnon" of the Rocky Mountains, Col. Robert Vaughn, Agent for the Blackfeet tribe agency, which was then comprised of 5 bands of Indians viz. the 'Bloods, Piegans, Blackfeet, Grosventres of the River and Grosventres of the prairie, who at that time gave their White Brother no trouble more than to set him a-foot — and it stood you in hand to look well to your Horses — gave us a royal Breakfast which was highly relished by all.

"The large Fry Pan piled up high with smoking steaks of Fat 'Big Horn' Sheep and antelope, good strong Coffee and Hard Tack — I'm sure it left a green spot in my Memory that will take years to efface, for I believe there is nobody but a hungry Man in the Mountains who can appreciate a Wild Meat Meal

We rested with the Hospitable Col. that day and enjoyed ourselves much, to hear MacDonald and the venerable Col. exchange stories. So, after a good days rest we were ready for saddle once more. We concluded on account of camping facilities to follow Sun River, to its mouth which we made in one day; thence along the high prairies following the meanderings of the Missouri River to the "Grand Coulee" crossing its mouth, and up again on the prairie over to the Buttes on top of the highland back of "Fort Benton" down the hill and up to the old adobe Fort Benton of the American Fur Company.

When the gate was opened and we were welcomed in the Fort by those in charge, Mr. Dawson being in St. Louis at the time. I believe DMichel Champagne, one of the traders, was in charge together with La Roche. Geo. Steel was Chief Clerk but I believe was down on the Missouri River somewhere on business for the Co., but we were treated fine. The Maj., Mr. McDonald and myself were given comfortable quarters; our Indians were also attended to, and our stock turned over to the Co's herders who would be responsible for their safe return when called for. Well, here is where I must tell a little joke on myself: At the Supper table I was given a seat next to Miss Champagne who had just returned from school at St. Louis, and who was a very pleasant conversationalist, and was to my surprise, dressed in the latest style — something I was not looking for — this far from Civilization, and me with moccasins and a long blue Hudson Bay over shirt did not correspond, but I soon overcame my bashfulness and entered into conversation. And, of course, I was hungry (one is most always hungry after riding Horse back all day long) with nothing but dried Buffalo Meat to eat. They had some very nice biscuit on the table, warm and light regular old fashioned ones like our Mothers used to bake, the first thing of the kind I had eat for quite a while, and I was probably a little wolfish with them. Anyhow, every now and then I would feel the Maj.'s foot nudging me and I supposed he meant for me to do the elegant and entertain the young Lady with small talk when I would reach over and take another biscuit, and another nudge from the Maj, and another biscuit; well, after supper I found out what the Maj's nudges meant for when he told me I had eat his and the young Ladies and several of the others' biscuits, as we were allowed one biscuit each, and I should have eaten only one, my share but as it was I was ahead considerable.

The next night Captain Malcolm Clark came down from the upper

Fort (there were two Forts at Benton at that time. The upper one, I believe, was owned by Frost Todd and Co. of St. Louis, with Capt. Clark in charge) to have a dance and brought the Ladies along, which together with those in the American Co's Fort made sufficient for a good sized Ball. Our orchestra was composed of one Fiddle, Dutch Jake; the Co's tailor was the Musician with the aid of a half breed boy to drum on a tin kettle for an accompanyment which made a pretty fair band, and by which we danced till the wee small hours and then retired, delighted with our nights entertainment at Fort Benton.

After a rest of 3 or 4 days we had the animals drove up and prepared for our return trip Home to the Bitter Root. When everything was ready and packed, saddled up and mounted, I reluctantly turned my back to Benton's old adobe walls and grand old Missouri flowing silently, beautifully and swiftly on its way to the Atlantic and often think of the pleasant hours passed within those old walls.

I very nearly forgot to mention the curtesy and favors shown us by the Head Chief of the Blackfeet "Little Dog." I presume he has gone to the happy Hunting Grounds ere this but our party was under obligations to him.

Capt. Clark accompanied us to our first days short drive from the Fort to the "Teton" and camped with us for the night, and the next morning we bade him adieu and watched him dash across the prarie on his Buffalo Horse towards the Fort whilst we headed for Sun River.

From Sun River we followed the trail for Little Blackfoot Pass of the Rocky Mountains. That day we made Bird Tail Rock and camped; the night bitter cold, Billy Rodgers and little Eanias half bloods from the Bitter Root valley came to our camp on their way to Benton. The Maj. paid our Indian packers a skin (equal to $2) per hour to keep a Fire burning all night; wood scarce, nothing but Willow twiggs. (sic) Would burn up faster than we could gather them; commenced snowing next morning, could not see the trail. Our party was not well acquainted with this trail, and, for a while we did not know which one of the boys we were until we sighted the Dearborn River and crossed. And from there on, all was serene, snow falling very thick and fast, nothing to disturb the Solemn stillness that prevailed but the occassional song from one of our Indians, and the low moaning of the winds through the Forest over Medicine Rock mountain at that time, with no one to molest it as the old trappers and Pioneers did not look on such things as curiosities. There was a large and varied assortment of Indian trinkets lying scattered around this great Indian "Hoodoo" known as Medicine Rock. Tonight we camped in the Prickly Pear Creek Valley. Here is the winter hunting camp of a man named Morgan who had a Blackfoot woman for a wife — the only white man we have seen on the road so far.

Today's drive will take us over the main Divide of the Rockies on to the Head waters of the Little Blackfoot river where we camp after a tedious days tramp through the snow which was about 2 feet deep on the divide. Today we will make the Hell Gate River. As we cross the low rolling hills after leaving the little Blackfoot and night fast approaching, we are greeted with a beautiful sight. There along the Hell Gate just above where the trails cross, to and near the mouth of Gold (or Pennetse's Creek) was the Buffalo camp returning Home from their Hunt, about 150 Lodges: Flatheads, Upper and Lower Pend' d'Oreilles' Kootenai's, Spokans, and Nez Perces. And here is where I first discovered that the Indian had considerable pride and it happened in this wise: The Maj. wanted to camp near the Chief Palchenos Lodge and so instructed Francoise; while the Indians were taking the packs and saddles off the Flathead Chief Kooyese invited the Maj. and myself in his Lodge until our Lodge was put up and things properly arranged. And after sitting in the old Chief's Lodge and warming myself nicely and as I thought long enough for the Indian to have our Lodge ready I went out to see about it, and lo and behold, nothing done. There lay the Lodge and poles packs and everything just thrown down on the snow and no Mr. Indian, I found Francoise the Interpreter and asked him the meaning of this, why the Lodge was not put up when he told me the young Men were ashamed to do Woman's Work, and especially where there were so many young women present. I then had Francoise to request of the "Chief" to order our Lodge put up, which he did, and in a very few moments there was a dozen Indian women to work, and had everything arranged in good order; brought wood, started Fire, etc.

In the evening the door of our Lodge was quietly raised and several fresh Venison Hams thrown in, which was very acceptable and highly appreciated by your writer, as I had got tired of chawing old Buffalo Bull Meat dried.

Well, now we will follow the Camp to Fort Owen, as the Ice in the

Hell Gate River is bad so we let the Big Camp dragging thousands of Lodge poles and driving some 3 or 4 thousand loose Horses go ahead and break the trail and Ice at the 13 crossings of the River as the trail then kept down the Canyon and crossed the stream about 13 or 14 times between Flint Creek and the Mouth of the Big Blackfoot. After several days of sliding and packing with frozen rigging we get out in the broad valley of the Hell Gate Ronde, and, as I remarked before, there were no settlers but the one, Mr. Brooks, to my recollection.

Across the Hell Gate and on our way to Home, Fort Owen, on up the beautiful Bitter Root valley, the Snow Crisp Cold but Clear and calm.

Today we are to reach our journey's end, and the Indians have all, old and young, decked themselves out with all the Indian Finery they possess for the occasion. And as the young Braves and Squaws prance along on their gaudy equipped Horses with bells and feathers in profusion, the sight was certainly picturesque and at last we dismount and each one to their quarters, to rest for the balance of the Winter.

This the 23rd of December 1858, and now if this little narrative will prove interesting to the readers of the "History of Montana" — the hardships experienced by its Pioneers, the great country they assisted in developing for the future Homes of thousands — I will feel happy indeed.

C. W. Frush

INDEX

COLOPHON

This edition of William and Charles Frush's, *THE OVERLAND JOURNALS* was printed in the workshop of Glen Adams located in Fairfield, Washington. Fairfield is located on State Highway 27 which runs between Opportunity and Tekoa, Washington and is one township removed from the Idaho state line. In this book we have combined three booklets by Charles and William Frush into one book. This book was started many years ago and has been worked on by many employees over the years. Recent typesetting was done by Garry Adams and Teresa Moore. Photography and film stripping was done by Dustin Newlun who also burned the printing plates. Printing was done by Trevor Del Medico using a Heidelberg press, model KORS. Folding was done by Garry Adams using a Baum Dial-O-Matic 26x40, three stage folding machine. Paper copies were bound by Garry Adams using a Mark II Sulby adhesive binding machine. Hard case binding was done by Al Chidester of *Arts and Crafts Book Bindery* in Oakesdale, Washington.